Reframe

Reframe

How Curiosity & Literacy Can Redefine Us

Tinsley Galyean

BEP

BUSINESS EXPERT PRESS

Leader in applied, concise business books

Reframe: How Curiosity & Literacy Can Redefine Us

Copyright © Tinsley A. Galyean, 2026.

Cover design by Geoffrey Beatty

Interior design by S4Carlisle Publishing Services, Chennai, India

First published in 2025 by
Business Expert Press, LLC
222 East 46th Street, New York, NY 10017
www.businessexpertpress.com

ISBN-13: 978-1-63742-922-8 (hardcover)
ISBN-13: 978-1-63742-880-1 (paperback)
ISBN-13: 978-1-63742-881-8 (e-book)

Service Systems and Information for Business and Society Collection

First edition: 2025

10 9 8 7 6 5 4 3 2 1

EU SAFETY REPRESENTATIVE
Mare Nostrum Group B.V.
Mauritskade 21D
1091 GC Amsterdam
The Netherlands
gpsr@mare-nostrum.co.uk

Description

In 2014, a small group of researchers began studying the possibility of teaching kids across the globe to read using inexpensive smartphones and specially designed apps. If their methods proved effective, could illiteracy eventually be eradicated globally? Could generations of humans attain the empowerment and opportunities that reading provides? *Reframe* is an answer to those questions.

In *Reframe*—part travel memoir, part spiritual journey, and mostly a recipe for prosocial success—Tinsley Galyean guides us through his odyssey to create and grow an international nonprofit organization focused on "giving everyone the opportunity to learn to read." Along the way, he discovers that what often blocks us from reaching our goals resides in our own minds—the beliefs we hold that limit our ability to see clearly. Examples from his own experiences provide tools for ferreting out these "limiting beliefs" and reframing them. Galyean demonstrates a process that allows us to free ourselves from the family and social conditioning that can blind us to what is possible.

Through personal narrative and data-driven analysis, *Reframe* transports readers across the globe—to India, South Africa, Bangladesh, Ethiopia, and Peru—where, through collaboration with parents and local partners, children awaken to new ways of learning to read.

On a quest for positive change, *Reframe* journeys inward and outward, across earth's terrain and the terrain of our vital relationships with ourselves and others. In short, this book is about the magic of curiosity and how it can free us from our own limitations and align us with a life of learning and growing—the true nature of success.

If you aim to live a more full life, lead an organization into uncharted territory, or just read stories that will change your worldview, this book has something for you.

Why Is This Book Needed Now?

We live at a unique time in history, when the world faces not one but many global challenges. Economic flattening, climate change, water security, migration, and immigration are all examples of global issues that can only be addressed by moving toward a unified world—what I would call a state of unity consciousness. These issues exert profound pressures on the global system, pressures that necessitate change. And all of this is happening in the midst of a technological revolution. We must respond to these pressures first by transforming ourselves. Next, we can address the needs of our organizations and, finally, the entire world.

The challenges we face as a global community have inspired a burgeoning interest in businesses that act for the social good—from double bottom lines to B Corps to hybrid nonprofit-for profits to social entrepreneurship. For those of us striving to work for the greater good, transformation begins when we identify the ways in which our own beliefs are holding us back; once we have done that, we can reframe limiting beliefs within ourselves and within our organizations. *Reframe* describes this process of transformation and provides tools for its implementation on multiple levels—personal, organizational, and global.

Contents

List of figures

Acknowledgments

We have something to learn from every person, from every interaction. When I and my colleagues stepped into the parts of this world that are furthest from our own experience, with the goal of realizing the Curious Learning mission of giving everyone the opportunity to learn to read, we opened ourselves to this reality. From the small NGO (nongovernmental organization) founder, to the World Bank researcher, to the donors that support the work, to the children and mothers in Ethiopia, Uganda, South Africa, India, and Peru—this work and this book would not have been possible without our connections. Those who we set out to help are the very same people who taught me what I needed to know to create this book. It would be impossible to even try to list all of these people. Below is my meager attempt to acknowledge those who were obviously and regularly present in the process. But the impact of those not listed was no less significant.

Nicole Goott, my wife and life partner, has supported me in more ways than can be listed here. To only mention a few: discussion partner, first reader, idea challenger, cheerleader. She is a published author in her own right and forged a path for me to follow and learn from. In short, writing (for that matter, life as a whole) is better with her. I am forever grateful for the opportunity to learn and grow together; this book is one example of that learning and growing.

Stephanie Gottwald is, first and foremost, my cofounder at Curious Learning. Curious Learning would not have happened had our unique set of skills and backgrounds not mixed to make it a reality. Thank you for the many travel hours we spent together, days sitting on classroom floors observing, evening reflections on what we did and did not see and learn, and the discussions that shaped our understanding of what was possible and revealed what we did not understand. And thank you for the research and field notes that supported the writing itself.

Curious Learning staff has grown into a remarkable set of people living and working around the world, each with their own experiences and worldviews. Many of them have directly or indirectly influenced this work. Creesen Naicker, thank you for your enthusiastic energy to talk about the latest stumbling block and eagerness to identify the beliefs behind it. Thank you, Ben Burrage, Deborah Oduman, George Dzavashvili, Jeff Oberlander, to name a few of the staff, for not only keeping the train running but also for patiently listening and adjusting as I presented new ways to think and operate.

The Curious Learning board—Miles Lasater, Nazia Kahlon, Mots Ehouman, Guru Banavar, Robin Morris, David O'Connor—is a wonderful and insightful set of individuals who are able to manifest that rare quality of challenging the status quo without being competitive or judgmental. They brought this quality as early readers of the manuscript. Miles and David in particular supported the process of getting to publication.

To other early readers and supporters of Curious Learning's work— Larry and Pam Tarica, Karl Bandtel and Farley Urmston, and Marni Grossman—thank you for the many rich and enlightening conversations.

I find it difficult to work, in particular to write, in a vacuum. To those early readers not mentioned, in particular Tinsley Kim, who also served as an early editor, thank you.

My good friend Kurt Leland, a multiple-time author himself, guided my work on many levels: by sharing his own writing and publishing experiences and, more profoundly, by engaging in many deep conversations about the nature of reality and the role of limiting beliefs in our lives. For those who know Kurt, they will, from time to time, hear echoes of his words in my writing. The nature of this deep friendship makes it impossible to give credit to every thought where credit is due, but please know how profound his influence has been.

Katherine Klutznick, editor extraordinaire, applied her amazing ability to see where clarity was lacking and sculpt the changes needed to bring that clarity, all the while staying in the tone and tenor of my voice. A true writing chameleon who works for the greater good with no ego. Rare indeed.

One last call out to all those children who have allowed us to try new ideas with them and who, by just being curious, help us reframe our own limiting beliefs.

Introduction

On a spring day in 2013, I was sitting in the atrium of the Media Lab at Massachusetts Institute of Technology (MIT). I had been there all day, working on spreadsheets as students, professors, and researchers hurried by, buzzing with excitement for their work. The numbers on the spreadsheets I had been building came into focus just as something bigger began nagging at me, struggling for my attention. I turned away from the spreadsheets and lifted my gaze to large windows and a pale sky above the Charles River, allowing my mind to rise above the atrium's hum. Wispy clouds drifted by and began filling the sky. It hit me: Those clouds were a physical manifestation of a larger global energetic blanket that was revealing itself to me. A bright light shone through, and I recognized my unique position within this vast overlay.

Have you ever thought about moments in history when multiple people converge on the same idea, invention, or discovery? An energy or a power exists behind the fabric of certain thoughts, as if some sort of "global intention" were seeking form, striving to tear through that fabric to manifest itself in a reality larger than any one of us. Somehow, these thinkers collectively stumble upon an intention, sparking a vision of what is possible, with an understanding of their role in its fulfillment. Their discovery is followed by a process that is partially given to them and partially emerges out of them. At such confluences, notions become callings to play a larger role in a global intention that has infused the hopes, dreams, and thoughts of many with a new energy.

That spring day in 2013, I realized that I was in the right place at the right time, with many of the right skills to tap into one of these confluences, to guide a global intention to the ground. How could I not answer that call?

For the better part of two decades, I had been working in technology and media for a variety of companies—from small startups, to companies that went public, to large, established media giants. My work had been at the nexus of how technology and design can expand and enhance media experiences. More often than not, the design and development work I had been leading centered on creating educational materials for young audiences. However, now, I'd found myself at an inflection point, both personally and professionally, and had stepped away from this work to explore the next chapter in my life.

During this next chapter, I was fortunate enough to be asked by a dear friend to help launch a new nonprofit center—The Dalai Lama Center for Ethics and Transformative Values—at MIT. My personal studies in Buddhist philosophies, my entrepreneurial experience, my scientific background, and my connection to MIT, all conspired to bring me to this post. The center focuses on inquiry, dialogue, and education that are grounded in meaning-making and moral purpose on a global level. Joining this effort to launch The Dalai Lama Center brought me back to the MIT campus, where twenty years earlier I had completed a PhD in media arts and sciences.

While there this second time around, another old friend, this one at the Media Lab, was kind enough to offer me a teaching position. Thus, I had officially returned to the Media Lab in a world much altered from the pre-web early nineties. The Media Lab is an interdisciplinary research lab that is known for its work in human adaptability, human–computer interaction, education, communication, artistic creation and visualization, and designing technology for social good. Now, teaching rather than studying, I was free to explore the new research being done at this iconic lab.

One of the projects at the Media Lab that caught my attention was a small side project investigating a simple question: Could children learn to read by using apps on mobile devices alone? A small group of highly accomplished researchers[1] from MIT, Tufts University, and Georgia State University had worked with folks at the early education nonprofit One Laptop per Child to test this proposition in two remote villages in Ethiopia. A couple of months after I first met them, one researcher returned from a trip to Ethiopia having discovered that over the course of a year, children who had been using apps designed for reading acquisition were reading at roughly the same level as students in well-resourced

---

[1]Cynthia Breazeal (MIT), Maryanne Wolf and Stephanie Gottwald (Tufts University), and Robin Morris (Georgia State University)

kindergartens in the United States. These were astonishing results. Was this a fluke? Could it be replicated? If so, could a system be created to scale this approach? Just how big was the need?

After several days of pulling data from a variety of sources and industries, I built out and populated several spreadsheets to try to answer some of these questions. I found the following: At the time, about 1.25 billion people globally were unable to read. Seventy-five percent of these people were concentrated in two geographic areas: India and sub-Saharan Africa. The economic impact was a loss of more than US$1.2 trillion in global gross domestic product (GDP) annually. It was estimated that if 170 million people were to learn basic literacy skills (at a first-grade reading level), world poverty would be reduced by 12 percent.

At the same time, smartphones were already finding their way into these communities and prices were dropping fast. At these rates, most people on the planet would have a smartphone within the next couple of decades. People and organizations had begun to realize this, and, as a result, there were a number of education-technology efforts, like Wikipedia and Khan Academy, coming to fruition and growing rapidly. They provided wonderful resources for learning, but there was one striking similarity among almost all of them: To use them, you had to be able to read.

In 2014, after a year of following this small literacy project, my friend and colleague Stephanie Gottwald and I, along with a board of researchers, founded Curious Learning, a U.S.-based nonprofit organization with the mission of offering everyone the opportunity to learn to read. The ever-growing global base of smartphone technology provided the opportunity to realize our mission. In the first six years of operations we had worked to:

- Curate and cultivate the development of smartphone apps that children can use to learn to read.
- Make these apps available in the languages spoken in areas with the largest illiterate populations, as it is always better to learn to read in one's mother tongue.
- Collaborate with partners to get these apps in the hands of children everywhere.

- Build out the data infrastructure to continuously evaluate the effectiveness of the programs and the content in order to facilitate an ongoing cycle of improvement.

Technology companies and market demand were creating the infrastructure we needed to reach students. Growing techniques and knowledge for leveraging big data were providing the tools to measure impact and hold us accountable to our goals while adapting to learners. Last but not least, the recent neuroscience research on how the brain learns to read gave us great insight into what types of content to try first. We found ourselves at a nexus, a confluence of events and ideas, with the right researchers and thinkers to manifest a global intention that seemed to hover, waiting for our recognition and action.

Back to 2013 and that table in the atrium of the Media Lab where I had planted myself for a couple of days to do this analysis, I stared out the windows once again, reflecting on something Stephanie had said to me. She said, "It is very unusual for a literate parent to raise an illiterate child. Once someone realizes the significance of being literate, they will do everything in their power to pass that skill on." If we could get a whole generation of children reading, we could effectively inoculate the planet against illiteracy. It not only felt doable, but it felt doable within our lifetime.

Little did I know that stepping into this new opportunity to be of service would also fuel my own learning and growth and reveal some of my own self-imposed limitations.

This book is a chronicle of our work at Curious Learning—from establishing our mission to the journeys that carried us around the globe to research and assess our effectiveness in reaching children and helping them learn to read. Along the way, we inevitably stumbled upon challenges within our team, with partners in our work, and with the families we hoped to serve. We also discovered some surprising methods for reframing those challenges, transforming them into opportunities for deepening self-awareness, engaging in more effective communication, and achieving goals as an organization and as individuals.

Over time at Curious Learning, we began to think of challenges, especially moments in conversations when exploration and opportunities for innovation stall, as "cracks" we had fallen into. The origins of these cracks, we found, were often located at junctures where blinders had obscured our vision. These blinders generally consisted of beliefs we and/or society as a whole held that limited our scope of vision—the kinds of beliefs we all hold, whether or not we are aware of them, beliefs that require courage and clarity and openness to recognize and analyze.

Our work, both at Curious Learning and my own work in my own life, to recognize when we have tumbled into cracks and to understand how to identify and engage with the limiting beliefs that may have provoked our fall, is still very much a work in progress. The aim of this book is twofold: first, to offer a view of one organization's quest to address the puzzle of global illiteracy, and second, to provide insight into the interpersonal dynamics that have allowed our organization to function effectively.

You, reader, must use your own discernment, thinking critically about our story and hopefully discovering ways in which it resonates for you. Our own shadows, the cracks that we fall into, our most firmly held limiting beliefs, all can be the most elusive. My hope is that sharing our story will not only inspire those working to end illiteracy but will also encourage others, both individuals and organizations, to consider their own limiting beliefs and ways of transcending them.

34,000 Miles of Curiosity

How a Curious Mindset Can Reframe Everything

I believe we have something to learn from everyone, with every interaction. I have cultivated a relentless curiosity in approaching every situation, every person, open to discovering what I might learn. I have learned the most, perhaps, from illiterate children on the other side of the planet, who struggle to live on less than US$2 a day. I hope the stories from the many miles I have traveled will inspire curiosity in you, too.

In 2014, six months before we founded Curious Learning, my soon-to-be cofounder, Stephanie Gottwald, and I set off on a crazy trip. The early research from the MIT, Tufts, and Georgia State group, showing that children in two remote villages in Ethiopia had been able to gain literacy skills by using mobile devices with a curated set of apps alone, had inspired us and spurred lots of questions. Could these results be replicated in different countries, cultures, and situations? With more data from more locations, could we better understand what types of apps would most engage and promote the learning process? In other words, was it practical to use mobile devices to offer people everywhere opportunities to learn to read? We were convinced that smartphones would become prevalent, and we wanted to be prepared to leverage them for literacy learning.

On our trip, we intended to follow up on the group's research, visiting and setting up more sites to begin the process of answering these questions. In hindsight, our itinerary was insane. We had scheduled ourselves to visit five countries—Uganda, Ethiopia, South Africa, India, and Bangladesh—by taking fourteen flights to set up or visit ten research sites. It amounted to 34,000 miles of travel in only twenty-eight days. All of this was to satisfy our curiosity. Benefits of this admittedly insane and unsustainable travel schedule were that it allowed us to experience a whirlwind of engagement with some of the poorest communities across the globe, and it allowed us to not only understand important issues but also to identify opportunities for transformation by observing similarities and differences among communities in rapid succession.

We had been planning this trip for more than six months and had partners on the ground in every location. With the help of our local partners, we would fly in and spend three or four days in each community, attempting to better understand their living conditions and talking through how we would set up research studies and provide kids with the apps that would help them learn to read. Our partners included:

- A woman on the edge of Kampala, Uganda, who had converted her home into a preschool for kids.[2]
- Two young entrepreneurs in Ethiopia who would be working with us in the villages.[3]
- A corporate foundation in South Africa working in government schools in KwaZulu-Natal.
- Several small NGOs in India that were working with impoverished communities in urban and rural settings.
- A British school teacher who, after a trip to Bangladesh, had decided to move to Dhaka to set up a small learning center on the edge of the urban slums to help the children living there.

In all cases, these partners were reaching children for whom the school systems were failing.

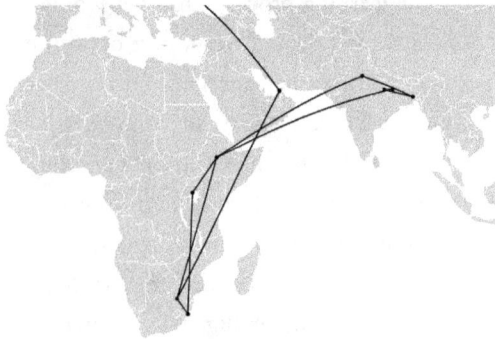

Figure 1: Map with travel lines that show the journey through Africa and India.

---

[2]We found her through a group of Americans who had started a small nonprofit to support her work. http://clover-foundation.org.
[3]With support from the Italian embassy.

Curiosity Without Expectations

Day 15: 16,177 miles
Kushinagar

We arrived in Kushinagar after a long day of driving (more accurately, being driven, but I will save the discussion about driving in India for later). Kushinagar is in northern India, just south of the Nepalese border, and it is a pilgrimage site where the historical Buddha died. There are a number of temples and hotels to accommodate visitors, which made it a good place for us to spend a night before heading into the countryside in the morning. We had a few hours before sunset and took the opportunity to walk to a few temples. As in much of India, the streets were lined with vendors, some selling fruit and vegetables, others selling services. We stopped for a few minutes to watch a man on the side of the road who had set up an ironing service. He had a small fire going on the ground, a large iron, and a hopper to hold coals. He transferred the red-hot coals into the iron then slid the iron across a pair of pants he had spread on a table. To my amazement, he did this without burning holes in the fabric or getting soot or dirt from the road on the pants. This ironing man had developed a surprising method that unexpectedly worked, a method that emerged out of tenacity, ingenuity, and necessity. Creative methods like this one are visible throughout India.

As we entered the temples, there were relatively few visitors, by Indian standards. I suspect this was in part due to the heat, which hovered somewhere around 47°C (116°F). Making our way to the famous reclining Buddha, a calmness filled the air. I felt as though this atmosphere of reverence, acceptance, and serenity had arisen millennia ago out of the Buddha himself as he left his physical form, and has been continuously reinforced by countless visitors from then until today. Every time I visit India, I am struck by the richness of the ancient wisdom that is embedded in the land, air, and culture and how it stands in sharp contrast to the scope and scale of poverty—the kind of poverty where one's basic physical needs are not met.

On our way back to the guesthouse, we stopped to bargain for a bag of mangoes. If you find yourself in India during mango season, I highly recommend that you partake. The guesthouse advertised air conditioning in at least some of the rooms. The window units were old enough that one would be forgiven for thinking they had been left there by the Buddha and his buddies. Needless to say, they clanked a lot as they struggled to do their work, which was just enough to make the heat manageable at night. After breakfast the next morning, we had a one-hour drive on mostly dirt roads to our destination, a small village in the northwest corner of Bihar, where we would meet our host.

Day 16: 16,187 miles
Baniya Chhapar

The small village of Baniya Chhapar in Bihar was the ancestral home of our host Surya Prakash Rai's family. He now lived in Patna and had driven up to meet us. In previous years, his small NGO had focused on bringing tuberculosis (TB) treatments to the community. TB treatment is a long and extensive process; providing the drugs alone is not sufficient. Successful interventions are a process of educating people and putting systems in place that support long-term compliance. Having successfully navigated this effort, Surya was now turning his attention toward helping with their education. We were visiting Baniya Chhapar to understand how we might make mobile devices with apps available to this community.

In spite of the heat, we were looking forward to another day of observing and learning in this remote community. As we pulled up to the village, we were surprised to see that they had set up a large tent. By this time, the temperature was climbing again after modestly dropping throughout the night. I figured the tent was another mechanism for providing much-needed shade, but quickly learned that this community was so excited about our visit that they had not only set up the tent but also a small stage at one end of it to facilitate our visit. It wasn't long after we got out of the car that we were shepherded to the stage and offered seats as honored guests.

We sat there for hours as different groups from the village performed or spoke in celebration of our arrival. We sat, dripping in the sweltering heat, watching the children of the village sing and dance on our behalf. They were all so excited about our presence. They had set up two large fans to blow air onto the stage. These old fans were special and were positioned to benefit us—their special guests. During our visit, we only encountered a couple of other fans in the village, those in the more affluent homes, and they only ran for the few hours a day that they had electricity.

Meanwhile, we could hear the thump of a gas generator in the background, providing power for the fans and an ancient Public Address system. The use of fuel to generate electricity was another indicator that this was a special event. Just to my right on the floor of the stage was a power strip that was connected to the generator. This power strip, like all the components, had seen better days. More importantly, it was not large enough for all the equipment they had plugged into it. They had cut the plugs off the ends of some of the cords and wrapped the bare wire around the prongs of another plug. This allowed them to "plug in" more than one item into each socket. This jury-rigged mess should never have worked with any reliability, but it did, like so many things here.

My discomfort grew as performance after performance and greeting after greeting dragged on. I was certainly hot and dehydrated, dripping with sweat, but I realized my discomfort wasn't actually physical (or fear of an electrical fire so close to my feet). What was it then? What was it that was making me so uncomfortable sitting on that stage as an honored guest in this village?

I only partially figured it out at the time. As I have reflected over the years, I have concluded that it came down to concern over how little I knew. Here I was, an honored guest who was expected to have insights and bring tremendous knowledge, support, and help to these welcoming people. Yet, as I sat on that stage, I realized how little I knew about the villagers' lives. How did they feel about education, their ambitions, and how they lived? What had they wrestled with in their lives? Maybe I felt guilty, or just plain disappointed, that I couldn't provide them with what they wanted from me. Then again, maybe it was that I knew there was real work to do and I had lots to learn, and I didn't think sitting on the stage would help. I expected to sit with and walk among these people, experiencing their daily lives, hoping to understand better how we could work with them and how we could be of support to their community. This is what we had been doing in other communities on this extended trip.

By many standards, Stephanie and I had a wealth of knowledge. Between us, we had decades worth of work in technology, designing and building better user experiences, research on how the brain learns to read, a deep understanding of the skills required for literacy, as well as the linguistic background to understand how that process could be adjusted or changed across different languages. But all these skills weren't enough. The adage, more like a cliché, "The more we learn, the less we know," was true for us in this context. Our trip was proving it every day. Spending time in the village with the children and families was the way we expected to deepen our understanding; sitting on that stage did not feel like it was getting us any closer to our goals.

The festivities neared their end. With our host's help as a translator, I was asked to take the mic and say a few words. I had no idea what to say. Fortunately, as the translator did his work, the lag afforded me a little extra time to push through the fog of the heat and come up with something to say. With considerable concentration, I expressed our gratitude and briefly explained that the tablets loaded with apps to help the children learn would be made available for them to use in the afternoons and that we hoped this would help them become better readers. I thanked them for being a part of this program and for helping us better understand how apps could help other children's educational journeys.

We left the stage and toured among the villagers and their community. They greeted us with great kindness and great curiosity. At one point, one of their spiritual leaders insisted on blessing us and giving us small handfuls of sugar. Some Indian traditions mark new beginnings with something sweet. By offering sugar as a puja at the temple and consuming it, you will be blessed with prosperity and happiness in your endeavors. Due to the language barrier, I was unable to confirm that this was his intention, but his insistence that we consume the sugar suggested so. The tour culminated in a meal at one of the more affluent homes in the village. Here, one of the community leaders explained how they would take care of the devices, where they would store them for safety, how they would charge them (with a generator they ran an hour or so every few days), and when and where children would come to use them on a regular basis.

As we walked through the details over lunch, I was awed by the extraordinary measures these people had taken in preparing for our visit. Our intention and desire were to be among the villagers as they went about the ordinary activities of their daily lives. Later in the day, I would come to realize the importance of this event, which had a larger purpose beyond our presence.

Our conversation continued, and hints came out that not everyone in the village was entirely on board with this opportunity. Some expressed resistance or, more likely, fear about this technology and approach to education. Our host dismissed this, as he had seen similar concerns he had managed to overcome as he brought TB treatment to the village. It was only later that I realized the morning festivities had not just been a celebration for honored guests—they were ways to build unity and excitement in the community for this new and different opportunity. This insight put my swirling thoughts, impatience, and, dare I say it, arrogance in their place.

My ideas about engaging my curiosity and learning were not what I expected. Being truly curious does not mean expressing your ideas of how to satisfy your own curiosity; it means being open and alert to what life brings you, remaining available to others by giving them the space to engage their curiosity. If this crazy idea of offering everyone the opportunity to learn to read was going to work, it would need to be a partnership in learning and growing—a collaboration among us, every child, every parent, and every community we reached. To progress on this project, we needed to embrace every moment, every person, with endless curiosity.

Letting Go of Judgment

Day 20: 21,477 miles
Addis Ababa

We arrived in Addis Ababa, Ethiopia, to visit our two oldest research sites, the first sites set up by the original research group, and the only two that had been running for more than a year. One was up in the mountains in a remote village, the other out in the bush. Our tasks were to check in, see how the villages were doing, and to observe firsthand how the mobile devices were being used. We would then begin the efforts to set up one or two more research sites in Ethiopia.

After a few days of visiting our first sites, we returned to Addis Ababa to clean up at our hotel and get ready to go to a senior Italian embassy staff member's house for dinner. Only a couple of days earlier, an Italian embassy member had accompanied us to the Ministry of Education to garner permission for additional research sites in the country. Ethiopia contains a number of culturally different groups, and political leadership is constantly jockeying to appear supportive of all of them. Because of this, the ministry had made it clear that our next research sites should be in the southwestern region of the country. The Italian embassy had been an instrumental partner in supporting our research sites.

You might wonder what the Italians have to do with it. Ethiopia is the only country in sub-Saharan Africa that was not fully colonized; the Italians made an attempt but failed after about five years—just long enough to construct a number of Italian-villa-inspired buildings at one intersection in the capital city. Though the colonial project failed, the Italian embassy maintains a significant presence, supporting a number of efforts in Ethiopia. They supported Curious Learning's early work, not only monetarily but also by streamlining the importing of devices by shipping them in diplomatic pouches.

In addition to supporting our work, the Italian government also supported other NGOs working in Ethiopia. One of those NGOs at the time had been working in southwestern Ethiopia. In addition to being more remote, this area was culturally different from the areas where we had already been working. Before we tried to set up new research sites in this region, it would be helpful to learn more about it and its people. The dinner at the senior staff member's home was an opportunity to do just that.

We passed through the home's security gate, and our host from the embassy welcomed us and introduced us to John Rowe, a photographer and filmmaker who had traveled extensively in the southern part of Ethiopia. John had helped his translator and friend, Lale Labuko, start an NGO that became the subject of one of John's films. After our host ensured I had a drink in my hand, it was not long before John and I were deep in conversation.

Like many NGO founders, John was passionate and very knowledgeable about his work. He explained that a large group in this region believed that certain children were cursed and that if they remained in the village they would bring more than bad luck. The villagers believed these children would bring suffering in many forms to their community. If a child's top teeth came in before their bottom teeth, that child was deemed cursed and was killed. If you have not heard of this practice, you are likely just as shocked as I was when I learned this was happening in the world. It took me a moment, but I managed to keep my reaction to myself and remain curious about what this man was telling me. He explained that this had been a long-time practice in this rural, remote community and, as a result, was generally accepted. With no idea how to change this behavior, I asked him how you even begin to shift a belief like that. He explained that their organization was setting up an orphanage and working to convince community leaders to allow cursed children to be raised there. This approach would not be easy. It was part of a long-term strategy that would start with saving the lives of these children, providing opportunities for them to grow up and live full lives away from the village.

My first gut-wrenching reaction was that this belief was barbaric. The idea that a child would be killed just because of how their teeth grew was appalling. Without taking the time to hear the perspectives of villagers or understand the NGO's approach, I immediately wanted to say, "NO! This must not be allowed. It has to stop!" This practice ran so counter to my belief system. But as I listened and asked questions, I realized this group was working smartly. By setting up an orphanage for these children and inviting the village to let them leave and be part of a different community, they were inviting the community to accept a different approach toward working within their belief system. The villagers could now extract the cursed child from their village, removing the burden without needing to kill the child. This NGO was trying to respect the beliefs of these villagers while suggesting an alternative action without judgment. The lack of judgment was key. No matter how egregious they felt this belief was, they chose not to judge this community for having it and, instead, offered an acceptable alternative.

This group chose to lead by example, demonstrating that they were not afraid of the curse and were willing to care for these children in their community orphanage. Their hope was that, over time, the villagers would see that these children were not suffering, perhaps that they had not been cursed after all. As these children grew up, their stories would provide evidence that might adjust the villagers' beliefs.

For me, there was an important lesson here: No matter how much another's beliefs run counter to our own, we must engage them without judgment. Judging others for their beliefs is counterproductive. We can instead work together to open new doors, to find new ways of thinking or believing. In this kind of collaboration, all parties choose which thresholds they cross.

This realization played into the final wording of our mission at Curious Learning, which is to give everyone the opportunity to learn to read. It's not to teach everyone to learn to read or to get everyone reading. The operative words are "give" and "opportunity." Our aim is to open the door and provide the tools and means for becoming literate without judging a person based on whether they decide to walk through that door or not. This is a subtle but important tenet that we have tried to continue to live by in our work.

Becoming literate is an act of empowerment that provides access to and understanding of information and services that otherwise wouldn't be available. But you can't force people to learn to read. Inviting someone to step into their own empowerment requires creating the space that allows them to choose to step into that power. Otherwise, you have disempowered them from the start. Meeting others with openness means meeting them where they are and not judging them for being in a different place than you are.

Curiosity Is a Prerequisite to Learning—Inside and Outside of School

Day 11: 16,032 miles
Varanasi

In Varanasi, India, our host was a colorful college professor, Dr. Rajani Kant. He was so filled with passion for his life's purpose of teaching that he couldn't help but see the kids running around the streets not attending school as students in need. In recent years, he had started his own small nonprofit, the Human Welfare Association, working with different communities to reach these children. Two of these communities were candidates for being research sites for our work. One of the more urban sites amounted to an open lot wedged between buildings in the Sarnath area. The second was a village about an hour outside Varanasi. We were scheduled to visit both.

Excited to get started, we asked Dr. Kant about our schedule for the next day. He explained that we wouldn't be able to visit the sites until afternoon, when their programs were running. Knowing his programs were outside the normal school schedule, I asked if children went to school earlier in the day. His shoulders slumped and his normally over-the-top enthusiasm disappeared. He explained that it was against the law to run his programs during school hours—officials feared his programs would be more engaging than school. They worried that children would ditch school and attend his programs instead.

He shook his head out of frustration and aggravation. This had been a point of contention for him for some time. "So, has government policy worked?" I asked. "Do the children indeed go to school in the morning?" He shook his head no. In India, there is a way people bob their heads as you talk to them that is somewhere between a yes and a no—it can mean either. In this case, the rest of the professor's body language conveyed an emphatic, "No."

Day 12: 16,037 miles
Sarnath

When we arrived at the first site in Sarnath, long woven mats had been set out in rows under a tree. There was only one small building, more like a shed, used by the teachers to store supplies. To my surprise, many kids were already sitting on the mats, ready for the teacher to start the lessons. It was a dry, hot day, and dust covered the children's bare feet and was kicked up wherever people walked. Dust, heat, the aroma of flowering plants, and the occasional smells of urine and petrol filled the air, as did incessant horn honking and the lilt of children's chattering and laughter. All combined to provide the unique smells and sounds of India. My understanding was that we had arrived early, well before the lessons were to begin, which would have given us time to experience the larger community. As we were introduced to the teacher, she confirmed that the start time of the lessons would not be for a while. She went on to explain that the kids often hung out there during the day instead of going to school; she had arrived early to meet us.

After a walk past the community well and visits with some of the locals in their homes, it was finally time to start the lessons. For what appeared to be an impromptu school meeting under a tree on an empty lot, the energy of the teachers and the kids was impressive. The children's eyes rarely left the teacher's face, and most were quick to throw their hands in the air or shout out an answer. When the teacher would ask for volunteers, there were always multiple takers. Over the years, during my visits to India, I have been to a number of schools, both private and public. By comparison, the children's engagement and enthusiasm were as strong as anywhere else, if not stronger.

Day 13: 16,067 miles
Outside Varanasi

The second village outside of Varanasi was a community we had not worked with before. They met us with similar enthusiasm, with kids and adults coming to sit under the tree to talk to us and express their excitement about this opportunity for their children. There was no talk of the role school played in their children's lives or how the new program would or would not interfere with school. In the years to come, as these two communities used mobile devices with the apps we recommended, we would see a similar level of engagement and learning as we had in our first communities in Ethiopia. Our host had decided to work outside the school system. This came with certain constraints, but, for him, they were worth overcoming. With respect to our own work, we wondered whether and how we might collaborate with schools.

———

Our visits to both of these communities raised important questions for us: Would our mission be best served by reaching children using apps inside or outside of school? Did we even need to answer that question? Could we design content and material that could be used under either circumstance? Over time, we concluded that we could. We now know that if we design and/or curate apps that are engaging and activate kids' curiosity to learn for themselves, these apps can be used either outside or inside the classroom.

To work outside the classroom, an app must engage the student first. A child's curiosity and excitement to play with an app need to be the driving forces for learning. Curiosity is a prerequisite to engagement; engagement is a prerequisite to learning. This kind of thinking is a departure from the traditional classroom education structure. The assumption is so often that, once you have a child in the classroom, you have a captive audience. You don't have to worry about being engaging. You, in essence, can mandate and oversee that they do the tasks required for the curriculum. The rare and special teacher understands the value of stimulating curiosity, which activates engagement. Both curiosity and engagement facilitate learning. These teachers exude enthusiasm and model curiosity, which inspires children to seek and question and learn with curiosity as well.

Some of us are fortunate enough to have experienced teachers and mentors like these—ones who spark us to engage our own minds in the learning process, ones who encourage us to enter our own self-motivated learning path. These are the people we reflect on throughout our lives, the ones who have inspired and enriched our learning journey.

This kind of curiosity and self-motivation is what we felt we needed to awaken and activate among children through this new medium. Could we do that? And could we do that at scale?

We were already seeing in Ethiopia that this medium, with the power of interactivity and gameplay, activated curiosity and was highly engaging. In years to come, one of the biggest nuts to crack would be how to get these highly engaging apps into the hands of kids. Would we work within traditional education systems like schools? Or would we find ways to access parents and children directly? What would the advantages and disadvantages of these channels be? Would one channel prove to be more scalable than the other?

Working Outside the Lines

Day 17: 16,330 miles
Kushinagar

Car travel in India is like very few other places in the world. Being a former British colony, the rule is to drive on the left-hand side of the road, but you would never guess that from firsthand experience of the roads there. If, in the rare case, you were to find yourself on a multilane divided road with a median, you would notice that about 20 percent of the traffic is on the wrong side of the road, barreling toward you head-on. Each driver takes the path they feel is their path of least resistance. Really, as a result, it feels like every path is of maximum resistance. It is more than disregard for the traffic rules; it is just the Indian way of driving. Because no one uses lanes, everyone honks. There has to be some system to indicate the location of other cars, and honking is it. So drivers honk not to express frustration but to let other drivers know where they are. This is so necessary that most trucks have a "please honk" sign posted on the back.

After arriving in Delhi, a friend of mine got in a cab to head to his destination. It was late at night, and there was a little less traffic on the road. The driver was going wherever he wanted with no regard for the road lines. Curious about what the driver was thinking, he asked why there were lines on the road. The driver replied, "You put them between your wheels so you can see better and stay on the road at night," which is exactly what he was doing at that moment. What was most astonishing about that answer was that the driver was totally serious; it was not a joke. I am still baffled by how a country can clamp down on a nonprofit providing educational opportunities to children for operating within school hours but make no effort to enforce road rules. They don't even ensure that drivers, in particular professional drivers, know the rules.

On one of our longer drives, from the Kushinagar area to Patna, I was riding in the front seat of a small car as our host, Surya Prakash Rai, drove. Though the trip was only about 200 kilometers, it took the better part of a day. We were on roads that were more rural, with only two lanes, one in each direction. No one adhered to the lanes, so a two-lane-wide road had traffic going in both directions, in both lanes! As hours of travel marched on and the lulls in conversation naturally grew longer, I began observing Surya's driving habits. There was the requisite honking every time we came up behind another car, but there was also the turn signal he kept using, even though we were not turning. After trying to discern the pattern for some time, I asked him about his methods. He explained that when a car was coming toward us head-on, he would turn on his blinker to let them know which side they should pass him on. There was no assumption that you always pass an oncoming car on a particular side. This needed to be negotiated by turning on your blinker and waiting for the oncoming car to turn theirs on to confirm the agreement. Or sometimes to indicate that they wanted the other side. This seemed insane to me. Something so simple had been made so complicated. All because there was no interest in knowing or living by the rules of the road.

In all the times I have traveled to India, I have never been in a car accident, and I have only seen them rarely. Is there an advantage to this method of driving? If so, what is it? There is certainly flexibility in beliefs about how to drive, and so drivers must pay close attention and meet all the other drivers without expectations of how they will behave. Every movement is an expression of an intention. Every turn of the steering wheel and press of a pedal has to be accompanied by listening and watching to understand the other drivers and their intentions. They are doing the same. All are free of beliefs about how things "should" be done. This allows everyone involved to experience immediate feedback and the repercussions of their actions.

In contrast, there is a stark difference between traffic safety and educational practices. Schools are built, students are expected to attend, and curricula are set and followed. There is very little opportunity to work or travel outside educational lines, and feedback is rare. When feedback is offered, it may be years or decades later, well after current students are out of the system and, therefore, too late to benefit them.

Within education, the lines become a metaphor for the beliefs, policies, and patterns of behavior that we all adhere to. We legislate, even mandate attending school. We dictate what needs to be taught at what grade level. We even specify the language of instruction. Every one of those beliefs is another line on the road that we must stay within. All this is wrapped up in the belief that this is the way it is done, because it is the way we have always done it.

But does staying within these lines get us where we want to be? Does it get us there safely, without harm to ourselves and others? It seems pretty clear in many middle- to low-income countries that we are not meeting our educational goals. So it seems time to question these lines and consider what it would mean to drive our education experience outside the lines. But taking that step is confounded by fear—fear that the new approach will be harmful instead of helpful; fear that change will not help educational results; fear that change will adversely affect those working in the current system; fear that change will improve educational results, redefine how education will work and, with that, upend the status quo. Those fears may be realized, and new approaches may fail to improve educational outcomes. We don't know if we will succeed, but we do know that the status quo will continue to fail the students.

But some are already flying in the face of convention, driving as if the lines have been erased, honking their horns in an effort to be heard and seen, praying they will not get run over before they reach their destination. A number of our hosts throughout this trip and other trips were some of those people. How can we support them? What tools and resources can we provide to improve their journeys and help them reach their destinations safely?

From Stagnation to Growth

Day 22: 21,570 miles
Wonchi

As we reached the remote village of Wonchi in Ethiopia, two children came running up the hill to greet us. It was no surprise that the boy in the lead was the one we had heard so much about. This was our first visit to the village, but others had told us his story. His father had committed suicide some years before. In this community, suicide is viewed extremely negatively and stigmatizes an entire family. The son had been shunned and barred from many of the village activities.

When our program was set up, we made it clear that every child in the village would get a tablet, with no exceptions. When the tablets were handed out, the children were told nothing about how to use them, not even how to turn them on. Within minutes, one child had figured out how to turn his tablet on and had already begun showing the other children. This child was our ostracized boy. Over the course of the first year of having the tablets, he was consistently figuring things out before the other children. He would share information with a couple of the older girls, who would then disseminate this new know-how to the rest of the children. Everyone knew this boy was the leader. When we asked how he was doing, he replied, "I am a lion." He now felt like he was on top of the world. This opportunity had redefined his relationship with the rest of the village as well as his relationship with himself. Over the course of this first year of the program, he had moved from surviving to thriving, from stagnation to growth. Having started their literacy learning journey, he and other children were now talking about the careers they could have, like working with computers or becoming doctors. Their whole outlook on what was possible had changed.

What was the reason for his transformation? Sure, our program provided an opportunity for him, but who is to say that was the cause of his growth? Some other opportunity could also have presented itself. After spending time with this boy and the other village members, I came to believe his profound change was a product of his natural curiosity, his curiosity about the tablet, about learning to read, and about how to share what he'd learned. By engaging his curiosity, he (if only momentarily at first) had left behind beliefs that had limited him, like the idea that he had nothing to add to his village. Or the belief that his father's suicide had condemned him to a life on the margins of his community, with limited resources. Curiosity is the antidote to stagnation, self-imposed or otherwise. Curiosity is the vehicle that moves us from stagnation to growth.

Driven by curiosity, we wield the ability to look beyond our own beliefs. We allow ourselves to try on other beliefs and see things from different perspectives. Curiosity knocks us out of our stagnated comfort, putting us back on a path of growing and thriving. Curiosity is so fundamental to this process that I think we often forget about it, take it for granted, similar to the way we forget that oxygen is fundamental to breathing.

In every child I met on this trip, I could see a glowing zest for life that many lose along the path into adulthood. Their innocent curiosity had not yet been covered up by the family and social conditioning that happens to all of us as we age. This knowing glow and supernatural energy are what make it so hard for us to look away from a young child's smile. When seeing that smile, we might ask if we ever had such a smile ourselves. Of course, we did! We have just taken on beliefs that suggest we should suppress that curiosity and that have the unintended consequence of removing the very oxygen we breathe, the basic instinct toward learning and growing. But there is a simple solution, if we can only remember it:

Just stay curious.

Curious about everything. Curious about everyone. Curious about what we have to learn from every situation, every emotion, and every person.

Fully Embracing Curious Learning

In only twenty-eight days, Stephanie and I had spent time with people in a variety of settings that included a floor of a one-car garage that had been converted into a classroom in Uganda, a straw-covered dirt floor in a high mountain village in Ethiopia, a half-constructed building with a small converted classroom in Dhaka, and a public school without running water in South Africa. The trip was unusual. We would land in a country, move through the resourced, amenity-rich structure of its international airport, then quickly transition to some of the more impoverished communities in that same country. After spending a few days immersed in those environments, we would move on to another country. All of the communities we visited had massive learning deficits. But this rapid, compressed style of travel allowed us to quickly identify the similarities and differences across five countries.

We noticed all the expected physical differences: various sizes and shapes of bodies, varied hues of skin. In addition, we experienced differences in physical environments, from high-mountain hailstorms on lush green hillsides, to over-the-top heat hovering over dry, brown plains. Social and cultural differences included religious beliefs, languages, and expressions—differences that were less pronounced among children.

Everywhere we went, we spent the majority of our time with children. What was most striking was how similar children were across national boundaries. They all liked to do what children everywhere do—run, skip, yell, hug, hang on to you, be read to. They all liked to play. But as anyone who has read about early childhood development knows, "play" is just another form of learning. At these young ages, we are built to learn no matter where we are born or how we are living. This was visible in the eyes of every child we had the opportunity to spend time with.

As I watched the eyes of the children while they played with their tablets, I could see they had become transfixed and immersed. Their energy, their demeanors seemed so uncomplicated and pure. But what was it exactly? Could I label it? Could I capture and cultivate this state of consciousness in myself and in others? I noticed a child raise a finger to her head in a posture of thought before lowering that finger to the screen to make a choice. She waited with anticipation for what would happen, what would change on the screen. A moment of realization would come. As I watched this cycle repeat itself over and over again, I saw spontaneous moments of joy that arose with each new gain in understanding.

When I looked straight into the eyes of these children, with nothing but curiosity, they would return that unwavering gaze. It was not a staring contest but a connection and a genuine transmission of mutual understanding. It was also an unspoken lesson that was gifted to me by them. In their gazes was pure curiosity, the curiosity that made them so full of life, this rich childhood curiosity that prevailed in spite of the extreme poverty that surrounded them.

I realized I was looking at uninhibited curiosity at work.

These children, when given the freedom to be themselves, had no preconceived notions or beliefs, no judgment about what should happen, no beliefs that they should or should not try one thing over another, no fear that their actions would lead to ruin.

Throughout our trip, we tried to follow their lead. To show up, be fully present. To ask questions with a genuine interest in their responses. We accepted them for who and where they were. This allowed us to learn from them, no matter who they were, how old they were, or what they did or did not know. It was a reminder that true curiosity is devoid of judgment, which includes judgment-free kindness for oneself and the capacity to be okay with not knowing everything. When an outcome is different from what you expected, it is not a failure but a moment of understanding. In this context, there is no such thing as failure, only learning.

A couple of months after returning from this trip, we had a decision to make. Would we take this work beyond a series of research sites? The natural next step would be to create a nonprofit organization devoted to our research and make that research available to the whole world. In many ways, this trip was designed to facilitate that decision. Was there enough potential to make this an endeavor worth committing our life's work to? For us, the answer was a resounding, "YES!" Besides the real possibility of catalyzing a massive positive impact on numerous lives, there was no doubt that we had much to learn from jumping in head first. As clear as we were about wanting to start this new nonprofit, we were equally clear that we would need to approach this endeavor with the same curiosity that we had learned to appreciate on this trip. We were and still are convinced that curiosity is the necessary ingredient for success.

Therefore, we set off to experience what it would be like to meet every moment, every opportunity, with curiosity, to explore how to create an organization that is based on the premise of curiosity. When it was time to pick a name, we chose "Curious Learning." This name spoke to the curiosity we wanted to activate in all the children we endeavored to reach. And at the same time, it also captured our need to stay curious ourselves, to facilitate our own learning. In other words, our goal became to provide the opportunity for everyone, including ourselves, to be curious learners.

The Journey Continues

These 34,000 miles launched a fascinating and curious journey to figure out how to give everyone the opportunity to learn to read, a journey that continues today. I have learned and will continue to learn much on this journey. But if I try to boil it down to the one most impactful thought, a starting point for everything I have learned to date, it would be as follows:

I aim to meet life with the endless curiosity that leads to learning.

To meet life with curiosity is one of the most profound ways to help oneself and others. This holds true in our multiple roles as individuals, family members, leaders, and global citizens.

We all inherit and collect beliefs over our lifetimes. Those beliefs frame how we act and react. They provide a foundation for how we move through the world. But sometimes those beliefs cause us to become stuck and stagnate. At times, they limit our ability to thrive. That stuckness limits our ability to reach our goals and keeps us from contributing to the greater good—for ourselves and others. Curiosity helps us realize that we are more than our beliefs. Cultivating curiosity allows us to learn in all circumstances, which in turn allows us to free ourselves from limiting beliefs.

The Art of Falling
into Cracks

Reframing Frustration as a Call for Curiosity

At our weekly team meeting, it was Director of Partnerships Creesen Naicker's turn to report on the twenty-plus meetings he'd had with different ministries of education throughout Africa.[4] He opened with, "We are between a rock and a hard place!" The exclamation point at the end of that statement did not indicate a sense of, "Oh, no!" His was an attitude of enthusiasm, more like, "Look what I found!"

In the preceding months, we had started shifting our thinking as a team. Over the years as a nonprofit, we'd had numerous meetings with all kinds of partners, all with the goal of giving everyone the opportunity to learn to read. Those meetings had often left us wondering why others were not seeing and engaging with the enormous potential that, to us, seemed self-evident. Were we delusional? Were they resistant to change? Did others know something we didn't? Did we see something they didn't? Maybe all of the above and more?

We suspected that we may have been finding some of the very same cracks that so many preliterate children around the world had already fallen through, the cracks that have allowed our world to contain 770 million completely illiterate adults and another 600 million children destined to join them. What if, instead of resisting these cracks, we allowed ourselves to fall into them, explore their depths? What might we find?

To do so, we would need to let go of judgment and engage these cracks with wonder and curiosity. We could ask questions that might help

---

[4]These meetings were the result of a partnership with UNESCO, in particular, our work with the Priority Africa and External Relations Sector.

us unearth the beliefs or issues they held. Now, we were actually seeking out cracks instead of avoiding or resisting them. Now, from within them, our team and partners were actively communicating with each other and with the cracks themselves.

Exploring Cracks

Creesen continued gleefully, "Do you know what the space between a rock and hard place is? It's a crack!" We had all just as gleefully come to see cracks as opportunities for further discovery and exploration.

So, how do we define cracks? Cracks are those moments in any conversation where exploration and opportunities for innovation are inhibited. In other words, those conversational dead-end streets, where everything comes to a screeching halt. This often happens when someone puts forward a dogmatic statement that shuts down further conversation, or when a thought arises in your own mind that does the same. As a result, you check out of the conversation. If you look closely at your thoughts at moments like that, you'll often notice that you feel stalled, stuck between a rock and a hard place.

Finding the Bottom

Once we had actively begun finding and exploring cracks, the next step was to figure out what was causing them. We started asking lots of questions. The trick was asking without judgment. Approaching a conversation with pure inquiry and a spirit of exploration helped diffuse any defensiveness. As people opened up, we asked even more questions. Our conversations naturally deepened, right down to the roots of our conversation partner's position.

At the bottoms of those cracks, we found beliefs that sparked resistance to new ideas. And this was true for ourselves as well. We needed to examine our own beliefs and articulate them. To the best of our ability, we needed to excavate our and others' beliefs, placing all of them on the table. In some cases, core beliefs are more widely held by societies as a whole or a segment of society. By inventorying all of our beliefs and, in some cases, assumptions, we realized that some beliefs were in contradiction with others. Individuals and societies often hold conflicting beliefs. When we expose such contradictions, things can get pretty uncomfortable. We naturally want to turn away from discomfort, so these conflicting beliefs can persist and leave us stuck in a kind of cognitive dissonance, which limits our ability to see beyond the crack we have created. In many cases, these beliefs directly or indirectly inhibit our ability to realize our goals. At Curious Learning, we started referring to these particular types of beliefs as limiting beliefs.

Our more recent meetings with ministries of education in sub-Saharan Africa had started to unearth a number of other limiting beliefs, the most recent of which was the ministries' belief that anything they did needed to be aligned with their official curriculum. They also wanted evidence that any new approach was effective. We came with evidence that our apps had a serious and meaningful positive impact on literacy skills, but the creation and curation of these apps had been based on the latest neuroscience of how the brain learns to read, not on curricula. At the time, in sub-Saharan Africa, only 12 percent of students read at grade level by fourth grade. That's 12 percent of all children enrolled in school. So the rock and the hard place was that ministries of education wanted evidence that the apps were both effective and aligned with their curricula. Their curricula, however, were not working. Studies were showing the apps were working, though. Changing the apps to be curriculum-aligned risked losing that effectiveness.

At the same time, we approached these meetings with our own beliefs. We felt that if we could just get these apps into the hands of children whose parents already had a smartphone, we could double the number of children who were learning to read. We speculated that this could be done for no more than the cost and time of sending a series of text messages to parents. The idea was that, for a very small investment, these apps could help solve a massive illiteracy issue. Why wouldn't governments embrace this remarkable opportunity? Why wouldn't they act quickly? We were naive to the political predicament they found themselves in and the ways their environment entrenched them in certain beliefs. It is the very nature (for good reason) of these governmental organizations to work slowly and with consensus. In other words, it takes time, patience, and a consistent effort to shift the beliefs of large organizations.

We discovered, too, how important it was to make sure our own limiting beliefs were not inhibiting this process for ourselves and others. To do this effectively, we first needed to identify our own limiting beliefs. So what might that process of finding a limiting belief look like, or what has our process looked like? It often starts with "falling into a crack" or "being between a rock and a hard place." Here are our steps for revealing our own limiting beliefs:

1. First, recognize that we are between a rock and a hard place or have fallen into the proverbial crack. Meet this newly discovered crack not with aggravation but with curiosity and a sense of exploration.
2. Begin to look at and enumerate all the beliefs in play. It is important to note that these are both ours and others' beliefs.
3. With all the beliefs on the table and inventoried, we start to inspect them. Are any beliefs in conflict with any other? Are any beliefs in conflict with our ability to reach our goals?
4. If there is even a hint of a conflict, we need to ask ourselves if these beliefs still hold value for us. Is there an experiment to be done that will test the validity or value of that belief? At this stage, we must be willing to examine the value of each belief. They may have had value once but now need to be reevaluated to determine if they still do or if they should be abandoned or transformed.

This process is not an easy one. It requires cultivating a strong sense of self-awareness.

We Are More than What We Believe

As we grow up, we become aware that we are not our bodies, that there is more to us than just our physical form. Next, we realize that we are more than our feelings or emotions. We see that we have a mind that can be engaged, that can observe those feelings and move forward no matter how powerful our feelings may seem. With awareness of the mind comes awareness of our thinking and the ability to witness our thoughts, our mindstream. Eventually, we notice that we are more than our mind, that there are beliefs that we hold that structure our thoughts and guide what thoughts we most actively engage with. For this work, we need to go a step further; we need to realize we are more than our beliefs. This can be challenging because we often feel our beliefs define who we are. It can be unsettling to realize that we need to let go of parts of ourselves that we associate with our identity. If we experience ourselves as more than our beliefs, we can allow those beliefs to adapt and change. Those beliefs that may previously have held us back may instead support our continued learning and growth.

No Child Left Behind

You Can't Be Everything to Everyone, Nor Should You Try

In 2017, I was in Nasik, India, with a man who was taking me to see the bus he had converted into a mobile classroom. As we drove out of the city, I watched the crowded streets and the traffic. As I described from our Kushinagar trip, driving is a seminal part of the India travel experience. More correctly, riding, not driving, as it is rare that a foreigner would want to drive, no less be allowed to. Those in India who can afford to have drivers. Who wants to drive in this mayhem of cars never staying in their lanes, horns honking, trucks and cars loaded way past capacity, oncoming traffic on the wrong side of the road? After a while, you stop paying attention, because, if you did, you would be in a constant state of fear. Inevitably, you eventually give yourself over to the belief that you won't be in an accident unless it's your time to be in an accident.

As I settled into the drive, I watched as we passed a school. It was the time of day when school was letting out. Kids around nine years old flowed out of the building onto the street and piled into vehicles, many of them auto-rickshaws, for their ride home. An auto-rickshaw driver waited as kids piled into the back. At first glance, it looked like they were stacking themselves like cordwood—there were so many of them stuffed into such a small vehicle. I saw nothing but an arm here, a leg there, a head, a hand. I was incapable of discerning what part went with which body, which was made even harder by the fact that they were all wearing school uniforms with the same cut and color.

For those who have not traveled in India or Southeast Asia, an auto-rickshaw is a small, three-wheeled vehicle. The driver sits in the front steering with a pair of handlebars, not unlike a motorcycle. They usually have a bench seat in the back with enough room for two passengers and maybe even a little space behind the bench for a few packages. A windshield runs up in front of the driver and attaches to a frame that extends back holding a canopy over the passengers. For the most part, the sides are open and the dust and air from the street flow through as you ride. More often than not, you will see additional people standing on the backs of auto-rickshaws, their feet where the packages might go. They hold onto the frame with their bodies hanging off the back of the vehicle as it zooms off.

These drivers waiting outside the school had been hired by groups of parents to bring their children to and from school. A cluster of families hires a driver, so there might be fifteen or more kids piled into one of these auto-rickshaws made to carry two people. We would never see anything like this in the United States. Every kid would be in their own seat, there would be a limit on how many could ride in a vehicle, and, of course, everybody would be strapped in with seat belts. In India, despite the sheer volume of people and the huge disparity in wealth, parents, like parents everywhere, work to create opportunities for their kids. At least these children were going to school.

We were headed out of town to a community many would call a slum, where most of the kids don't go to school. Our host had gotten to know this community some years before and over time had gained their trust. He became convinced that the best way he could support the kids, the girls in particular, was to help provide them with the opportunity to learn. When his attempts to convince the community to send their kids to school failed, he took it upon himself to bring learning to them. He found a bus and converted it into a mobile classroom. He started by parking it several times a week at the edge of their community. At first, people were puzzled and no one came. But he brought the bus back time and time again, and, eventually, a few kids started showing up and parents allowed it. Over time, the whole community embraced it. Now, the bus only needed to pull up and kids quickly arrived, excited for the lessons and the experiences it provided.

Our host was excited to explore how digital learning tools might help this group of children. We pulled off on the side of the road and parked. It was a hot, dry day as we got out of the car and started our walk along the dusty road toward where the bus was parked on the edge of the community. Even from there, you could see the rows of corrugated metal, temporary homes that are so common in these types of communities.

If you looked carefully, you could see an entrance to a small latrine or cesspit, either wedged between a couple of the corrugated metal homes or at the end of a row. On a hot day like this, the odor reminded you of their presence.

Our host explained that many of the parents were day laborers or had small businesses, making on the order of one half to one lakh per year. A Lakh is 100,000 Indian rupees, so at the current exchange rate, this was between US$2 and US$4 a day.

We stepped onto the bus and joined the kids. Once the novelty of the foreign visitors subsided, we moved back into the bus to sit with the children and enjoy the lesson. These kids were truly engaged and showed real enthusiasm and excitement for the lessons and what they were learning. Our host had succeeded in making a real difference in these children's lives. When the lesson ended and we had spent the requisite time taking pictures of the children, then showing them their pictures, I stepped out to catch up with our host. I congratulated him and asked him why the school system had failed these children.

He explained that there was a school that these children could attend, but their parents were reluctant to let most of the children go. This was a particularly insular community, and it had taken him a great deal of time and effort to become accepted. These people had gotten along for generations with very few of them being educated, and so they were less accepting of change. In addition, parents were particularly concerned about the safety of their daughters. As soon as he mentioned this, I was reminded of seeing tight thread necklaces around the necks of some of the girls who were probably around eight or nine years old. I asked him about the significance of those necklaces. He explained they were a symbol that a girl had already been promised for betrothal. The color of the threads indicated to whom. He had realized that it wasn't his job to change their beliefs or their customs but to provide an opportunity for the children to learn and expand their understanding of what was possible, especially for the girls. His heart had been touched when he met the people in this community, and he was working to make sure no child was left behind. I had no idea how often I would come to hear the phrase "no child left behind" over the next few years.

In 2019, we were engaged in numerous discussions with NGOs, multilateral organizations, and governments. Those conversations consisted of explaining the Curious Learning approach and exploring how our approach could be applied and distributed to the populations these parties represented and worked with. By this time, we had curated and/or created a small collection of apps that helped develop early literacy skills. We had also shown the world how these apps could be rapidly localized into forty-eight different languages. It is generally accepted knowledge that it is better to learn to read in the language you speak before moving to a global language.[5]

Much of our work was and still is exploring how to distribute the apps. In other words, how do we get these apps into the hands of kids so that they can play with them and learn from them? We decided that the only way this would scale quickly and economically was to target existing parents' smartphones. So the approach was to ask our partners, NGOs, governments, or community-based organizations to run an information campaign to get parents who had smartphones to install the apps and encourage them to give them to their kids.

As we talked through this approach, it was not uncommon, in particular for the larger organizations, to bring up the phrase "no child left behind" at some point in the conversation. They wanted to know how this approach would reach the people they considered most vulnerable—those below the poverty level who likely did not have access to smartphones. Sometimes it was a genuine exploration of how this technique and technology could eventually reach everybody. But often the implication was: This is not for us unless it works for everyone.

To revisit the numbers, in 2019 we were looking at a world where 770 million adults were considered completely illiterate. On top of that, roughly another 600 million kids were destined to remain illiterate. Of those, more than 75 percent were concentrated in India and sub-Saharan Africa. This doesn't even take into account all the people who are considered literate but who have reached a level of literacy that is wholly inadequate. For example, in sub-Saharan Africa, only 12 percent of fourth

[5]H. Abadzi, *Efficient Learning for the Poor: Insights from the Frontier of Cognitive Neuroscience* (The World Bank, 2006).

grade students read at grade level. That means whatever educational interventions are going on now are only truly effective for about 12 percent of this population. So, any approach that can reach 24 percent of this population and help them learn to read could double the number of literate people in sub-Saharan Africa.[6]

Also in 2019, there were about 375 million smartphones[7] in India and about 360 million[8] in sub-Saharan Africa. Approximately 25 percent of the adult populations in both places already had smartphones. Projections suggested that there could be close to a billion smartphones in India and nearly 700 million in sub-Saharan Africa by 2025. In just six years, we could exist in a world where 50 to 75 percent of these populations have smartphones. In cultures where multiple generations live together in extended families, it's reasonable to think that an even larger percentage of homes would have a smartphone available.

When we heard this resistance to reaching out to families via smartphones, I started relying on an analogy. If there were a massive illness and you had a drug that could immediately cure 25 to 50 percent of the population, wouldn't you put that drug to work right away? Or would you shelve it because you weren't able to reach everybody immediately? The answer is obvious: It would be unethical to not make treatment available. The same is true in the case of illiteracy. For some, this was a powerful analogy, but, more often than not, they still did not feel empowered to act. In less than a year, we would be in the middle of a global pandemic, and this analogy would have a whole new weight, maybe hitting too close to home.

The small organizations that were in the trenches dealing directly with children and families were happy to jump on board. They were glad they

---

[6]UNESCO Institute for Statistics (UIS) and UNICEF, *Fixing the Broken Promise of Education for All: Findings from the Global Initiative on Out-of-School Children* (UIS, 2015).

[7]S. Rai, "India Just Crossed 1 Billion Mobile Subscribers Milestone and the Excitement's Just Beginning," *Forbes,* January 6, 2016, http://www.forbes.com /sites/saritharai/2016/01/06/india-just-crossed-1-billion-mobile-subscribers -milestone-and-the-excitements-just-beginning/#1d459ed65ac2.

[8]Pew Research Center, "Social Media Use Continues to Rise in Developing Countries, but Plateaus Across Developed Ones", June, 2018, https://www .pewresearch.org/global/wp-content/uploads/sites/2/2018/06/Pew-Research -Center-Global-Tech-Social-Media-Use-2018.06.19.pdf,

had something that could help at least part of their population while they figured out what to do next. But the larger, more political organizations were often unwilling to take the political risk associated with not helping everyone. In other words, they were willing to let "no child left behind" become the excuse for why they were willing to "leave all children behind."

I would argue that the true intent of "no child left behind" is to do everything we can to help those we can now, while also pledging to work to reach everyone else as soon as possible. That meant running our campaign and getting the message out to all parents or caregivers who had smartphones and then continuing to work to find ways to get smartphones to others. One way to do this would be by subsidizing and handing them out preloaded with the content. These were ideas that we and others like the World Bank were exploring. But why wait until we could reach everyone? We wanted to get what we could out to those we could reach at that moment. If we didn't, we were at risk of losing yet another generation of kids to illiteracy. When 88 percent of a population is not reading at grade level, we have an epidemic.

There was also an economic argument for reaching everyone we could then. Our tests had suggested that you could run an information campaign that would cost anywhere from about ten to twenty cents to acquire a learner. In other words, the cost of running the campaign divided by the number of kids who would actually end up using the apps for learning happened to be about ten to twenty cents. To give some context, in the United States in 2019, the average school district spent approximately US$10,000 a year per child to provide them education. In low-income countries, that expenditure ranges from around US$200 to US$1,000 per child per year.[9] So, for less than a tenth of a percent of an education budget, you can provide this foundational educational skill to a significant portion of your population. This leaves an enormous amount of financial resources to reach the balance of your population and provide other services.

———

[9]OECD, *Education at a Glance 2020: OECD Indicators* (OECD Publishing, 2020).

Coming back to our community on the edge of Nasik, India, two years earlier. Were we at Curious Learning too early to help these kids? They didn't have what we would consider basic sanitary needs, and a family might only make US$2 to US$4 a day. How were a set of apps that worked even on low-end smartphones going to reach this population? Were we going to need to leave these children behind? Would we be allowing a generation of kids to grow up without the opportunity to learn to read from our apps, while we waited for the price of smartphones to drop to the point where these people could afford and embrace them?

My host waved me over. He wanted to show me something. We walked past several rows of housing and came to a small clearing. He said he thought he could build a kiosk there and provide phones or tablets with apps installed. Children could visit and use them in place. I found this idea interesting and encouraged him to explore it. I let him know that our apps were free and that he could use them as he saw fit. I explained that we currently had an app in English and were at the beginning of localizing our apps to more languages, like those needed in communities like his all across India.

By this time, some of the parents had become curious. One of the fathers invited me into his one-room home. I stepped inside, and, with the help of some translation, I asked him about himself and his work. He told me he made turbans that people wore at their weddings. Excitedly, he reached into his pocket and pulled out a smartphone to show me pictures of the turbans he had made. Imagine my surprise—I had stepped over open sewage into a temporary structure that this man called home, only to have him unexpectedly prove my assumptions wrong—there actually were smartphones in the community. After a little more back and forth, I learned that the smartphone was well worth its cost for him—with it, he could stay in touch with his customers, and it allowed him to take photos that he could send to them. His smartphone had become an instrumental part of each transaction. I asked if he would be willing to let his children use the phone sometimes to play games that would help them learn. He demonstrated no lack of enthusiasm.

In 2017, we were only beginning our effort to localize apps into many different languages. This interaction, and many more to follow, encouraged us to pick up the pace on our work so we would be ready as smartphones became pervasive in the populations we most wanted to reach. We were unknowingly preparing for 2020, when a global pandemic would force nearly every child in the world out of school in a matter of weeks, a situation that would make our work all the more relevant.

Learning to Read

Celebrate Success Even When It Appears Different Than Expected

We were visiting a small village outside Varanasi, India, on our giant research trip in 2014. It was just before the monsoon season, and the village was dry, hot, and dusty. Most of the villagers were gathering under a tree to meet us. As we walked through the village, I noticed a woman sitting on the ground working; I wanted to understand what she was doing, so I stopped to watch her. She repeatedly picked up a thin, cut stick and rolled a clay-like material by hand onto it before laying it out to dry. She moved so quickly, she must have rolled hundreds of these in an hour. With the help of our host, I learned that she was hand-rolling sticks that would become incense, a common occupation for women in the neighboring communities. She would only have enough to sell once she had filled a large bag. The final step to completing the incense would be the addition of fragrant oils, but this would be done once the sticks were out of her hands. The oils are the most expensive ingredient by a lot, and the women were not entrusted with them. It would take a day-and-a-half to two days for her to produce this large bag of incense sticks. For that bag, she would receive around 100 rupees, or US$1.50.

Despite the extreme heat, the villagers gathered under a large tree with genuine interest and engagement. With the help of our host as a translator, we learned that they were very interested in the opportunity to have educational tablets in their community. They also had lots of good questions. In particular, some of the older women wanted to understand how the tablets would be used. We were well-received, as was the idea of bringing tablets to the village. This was in great part due to all of the work our host had been doing. He and his team had been working throughout villages and communities in this region, creating educational opportunities for both children and adults.

After the meeting under the tree, we were shown to one woman's home. This was the place where the tablets were to be stored and charged between uses by the kids. We entered a room with a dirt floor off one of the main courtyards of the village. This room was her living space in the evenings and a small shop during the day, where she sold snacks and some food staples. I noticed an old TV in the corner and asked about it. We learned that electricity came into the home, but was only on for an hour or two each day at random times. The woman left the TV on all the time so that when the power came on, people would gather around it and watch whatever they could for as long as they could. Tablets would be stored in this woman's space, so they could be charged whenever the power happened to come on.

We finished up our visit and started to walk back to the car. We were accompanied not just by our host but also by a representative of one of his funders. Her organization had been supporting a program he'd been running in a nearby village to help adult women learn to read. After talking to us and accompanying us on our visit to our research village, she asked if we'd be willing to visit the village she was supporting. She was interested in getting our opinion on the effectiveness of her program. She was concerned that the women were not making progress as quickly as they should.

This second village was very similar in size and socioeconomic structure to the previous village. There was one building that was used as a classroom. For this more traditional program, a teacher or facilitator would come to the classroom several times a week, and the women would gather for a couple of hours of instruction and practice. Our host was excited to explain that they had been running the program for about two years. When they first brought the program to the villages, there was some resistance, particularly from the men, who believed the women could not learn. Our partner had challenged those men and managed to negotiate a deal where most of them had agreed that if the women could learn numbers and basic literacy skills sufficient to use a cellphone, they would allow the women to have their own cellphones. Typically, only men owned phones.

After being greeted, we sat with the women and observed the lesson. They were being taught to read and write in Hindi, which is a more daunting task than learning to read in English, due to the complexity of

Devanagari script. While the women still had much to learn, we were impressed by what they could do. It was clear that the funder was not so impressed, feeling like the progress should have been more extensive over the two years of the program.

———

Learning to read is much more complicated than most of us realize or remember.[10] Typically, in a well-resourced community, like in many parts of the United States, a child spends approximately four years learning to read, between the ages of four and eight. Learning to read is the primary academic focus between kindergarten and third grade. You can think of it as having a full-time job for those four years. Why is it so difficult and demanding? And why do we not remember it as being so?

Over the past few decades, researchers have developed a deep understanding of the neuroscience behind learning to read.[11] We now understand that a rather extensive rewiring of the brain is necessary to build up the ability to look at a sequence of symbols and correlate them with both speaking the word and knowing its meaning. For example, on the left side of your brain, there is an area that for the first years of your life was activated whenever you saw a face and worked to remember the name of that person. As you start to learn to recognize the visual parts of letters, that part of the brain is taken over for this new skill. The ability to recognize faces migrates to the right side of your brain, rebuilding that ability in a new part of your gray matter. This is only one of many examples of what your brain went through over those four years of learning to read. This speaks not only to the amazing ability of the brain to be rewired (changing its neural pathways) but also to the complicated contortion your brain goes through to give you this amazing skill.

---

[10]M. Seidenberg, *Language at the Speed of Sight: How We Read, Why So Many Can't, and What Can Be Done About It* (Basic Books, 2017); M. Wolf and C. J. Stoodley, *Proust and the Squid: The Story and Science of the Reading Brain* (Harper, 2007).

[11]S. Dehaene, *Reading in the Brain: The New Science of How We Read* (Viking, 2009); Wolf and Stoodley, *Proust and the Squid*.

I don't think I fully appreciated the magnitude of this until my colleague explained the following to me. Oral language has been around for hundreds of thousands of years; our brains have evolved to the point that we are born ready to learn oral languages. You come out of the womb with much of the neurological structure needed to acquire oral language.[12] In contrast, the written word has only been around for several thousand years and has only been accessible to a large percentage of the population for hundreds of years. So, when you learn to read, you are repurposing (or rewiring) parts of your brain for a function (or really sets of functions) it was not born to do.[13] It is amazing and wonderful that our brains are capable of this.

For the sake of our work at Curious Learning, we have created a simplified list of the skills that are needed to learn to read. Those twenty-eight skills are listed in Figure 2 below for the English language, organized in eight categories across four reading levels. For the most part, the skills needed for reading are similar across languages, but there are a few that change in some languages. Chinese characters, for example, are visually more complex than Latin letters and represent syllables, not individual sounds. Thus, these characters are stored and processed slightly differently than Latin letters. However, all languages require children to develop highly sophisticated oral language skills and deep knowledge of the writing system to become proficient readers.

We have aligned the list of skills with four different reading levels and the U.S. grade level in which they are typically achieved. The process of mastering these skills is rarely this linear. It is common for a particular development of base skills to start while a child is simultaneously exposed to more challenging or consolidating skills. They will move back and forth among different skills, often returning to those earlier skills for refinement. The learning process is interactive and dynamic, and the expectation is that proficiency is achieved over the first four years of school. For many children in high-income countries, that is not always the case and is rarely true for children in lower-resourced environments like low-income countries. That is why we prefer to think about emerging readers at their

---

[12]M. Mahmoudzadeh, F. Wallois, G. Kongolo, S. Goudjil, and G. Dehaene-Lambertz, "Functional Maps at the Onset of Auditory Inputs in Very Early Pre-term Human Neonates," *Cerebral Cortex* 27, no. 4 (2017): 2500–12. https://doi.org/10.1093/cercor/bhw103.

[13]Dehaene, *Reading in the Brain.*

Pre-Reader
(U.S. Grade K)

Oral Language
- Vocabulary
- Sentence structure
- Background knowledge

Print Awareness
- Exposure to written language
- Recognizing symbols

Phonological Awareness
- Recognizing difference in sounds of words
- Number of sounds in words
- Syllables, rimes, and onsets

Emerging Reader
(U.S. Grade 1)

Letter Sound Knowledge
- Basic vowel/consonant patterns
- Letter combinations
- Letter pattern knowledge

Letter Names
- Letter names (only a few languages)

Consolidating Reader
(U.S. Grade 3)

Fluency
- Accuracy in word decoding
- Automticy in word recognition

Comprehension
- Advanced oral language knowledge
- Understanding action/text facts
- Identifying characters & plot
- Identifying sentence components
- Background knowledge
- Local text inference
- Global text inference

Early Reader
(U.S. Grade 2)

Decoding Skills
- Blending words
- Identifing rhyme patterns
- Advanced letter pattern knowledge
- Identifiying syllables
- Sight words

Vocabulary
- Word familes
- Sight word vocabulary

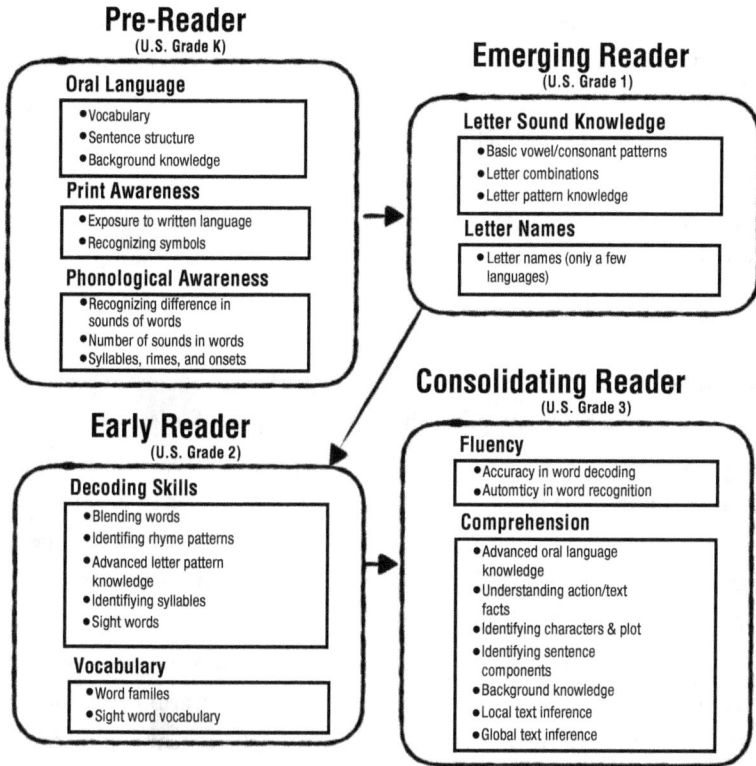

Figure 2: Diagram showing the four stages of becoming a proficient reader. Each stage lists the required skills for that stage.

skill level and not their age or grade level. This way, we are working to flesh out the needed skills independent of age or grade level.

You will notice that the first set of skills focus on oral language. Yet language learning—learning to speak a language—is different from learning to read. It is much easier to learn to read a language if you speak it first.[14] This is particularly true for the first language you learn to read. It makes sense if you think about it. If you learn the sounds a letter represents and start to sound out a word, you can effectively read the language, but you have no idea what you are saying. You need to be able to recognize the meaning of the word you just read. This is why the first few skills listed are oral language skills. It is also why it is better to learn to read in your mother

---

[14]K. Koda, "Reading and Language Learning: Crosslinguistic Constraints on Second Language Reading Development," *Language Learning* 57, no. 1 (2007): 1–44. https://doi.org/10.1111/0023-8333.101997010-il.

tongue, the language you speak first and at home. Then those reading skills can aid the process of learning a second language, both orally and in print.

Learning to read also involves environmental and cognitive factors that impact the ease with which children acquire this new skill. If you take any group of children from around the world, some will find learning to read easy, some will need more support, and others will struggle and need extra help. How does that break down in a typically well-resourced and educated population?

About 10 to 15 percent of children will learn to read by being exposed to reading material alone. This group is unusually curious about print and has an aptitude for figuring out the "code." Aptitude for learning how to read is similar to an aptitude for math or music or athletics. Each of these areas involves different skills, but we know that a small percentage of people show a natural talent. These people require exposure and time to practice, but they need less instruction to master skills. Exposure to oral language prior to school entry sets the stage for ease of learning. Children who happen to have an aptitude for learning to read, who have also been read to a great deal, and who have had rich, language-learning experiences are, unsurprisingly, the most likely to achieve high academic outcomes.

Another 55 to 60 percent of children will have little to no difficulty as long as they receive structured, systematic instruction and adequate support to develop the skills needed to read a language they already know. These children benefit greatly when they have broad and deep language skills similar to high achievers, but they simply have somewhat less aptitude for learning to read. Direct instruction in literacy skills allows them to gain the information about letters and sounds that they would not gain on their own. Poor instruction or less-than-ideal oral language skills make the transition from being a nonreader to an emerging reader more difficult.

The remaining 25 to 30 percent are children who will struggle more than most in some capacity. The most common reason for this difficulty in learning to read would likely be some form of reading disability or dyslexia. For many of these children, extended learning time with the material will help. For example, they may need to practice a skill two to three times longer than other children before mastery starts to kick in. If there is a game or activity that helps them develop and reinforce a skill, these children benefit from the opportunity to play the game or engage in the activity more often and for longer periods of time, according to their needs. The trick is to make sure the game holds their attention. So, having a collection of multiple activities for each skill keeps a larger percentage of children engaged and supported until they have become independent readers. In addition, it never hurts any child to practice a skill even after a level of mastery has been reached. In other words, what is good for children with dyslexia is good for all children learning to read.

The Curious Learning mission is to give everyone the opportunity to learn to read. We are guided by scientific research on how people become readers, and we take advantage of the advent and proliferation of mobile devices. As of the publication of this book, this is a high-level overview of our approach. We have never been tied to a particular piece of content or app. We are most interested in what works.

We curate apps that will eventually cover all twenty-four skills noted above. We think of this list of skills as a map, an "app map," and our job is to fully populate this map. To that end, we focused initially on apps that cover the early skills in the pre-reader and emergent-reader categories and that would be simple to adapt into many different languages and cultures. We describe the process using the term "localization" instead of translation, because there is often more to it than merely translating the content of an app. Besides cultural or social references, like the word "bat" referring to both a baseball bat and a cricket bat (they look very different), learning to read requires a deep understanding of the writing system that represents the sounds and words specific to that language. The first words you learn to read in English (three-letter words with predictable letter–sound relationships) may not be simple words in other languages. It is then necessary to change the pool of words used in the app to reflect the "easy-to-read" words of the new language.

One of our first apps focuses on "letter–sound knowledge," an aspect of phonemic awareness, and is called Feed the Monster. In this app, kids feed their game monsters by matching sounds with letters, which helps them identify the sounds letters make and how to blend these sounds together to make words. This app, created by Apps Factory, was one of the winners of the EduApp4Syria contest. In addition to being very engaging, Feed the Monster has a number of qualities that make it ideal for localization. It also serves as an example of how apps could be designed for high impact in education. The gameplay and graphics are designed to be culturally neutral, meaning children from all over the world should be attracted to the game. We also often refer to Feed the Monster as being "lightweight." When you download the game, it doesn't take up much space, which is crucial for projects that use low-end smartphones that do not have very much memory. Feed the Monster was the ideal test case for our team to prove that it is possible to design apps that can quickly and efficiently be adapted to many languages.

Feed the Monster is also open-source, meaning there is no legal limitation to using the code or the content of the game to make new versions. Wherever possible, we choose to work with open-source apps. Open-source apps allow us or others at any point in the future to adjust and change the app and facilitate further localization and improvement. When the Digital Public Goods Alliance was launched, Feed the Monster was immediately included. It was recognized as an open-source digital asset supporting the United Nations Sustainable Development Goals (SDGs). These seventeen SDGs, adopted by all UN member-states in 2015, aim to improve health and education, reduce inequality, and spur economic growth globally. The fourth of these goals is to "ensure inclusive and equitable quality education and promote lifelong learning opportunities for all."[15] Feed the Monster was one of the first digital assets to be accepted as a Digital Public Good supporting Sustainable Development Goal Number 4.

As of 2024, we and partners have adapted Feed the Monster to more than fifty different languages and even other dialects—from Portuguese to Pashto, Tajik to Twi, Arabic to Amharic. Our collection includes five different varieties of English and two varieties of Portuguese; it is the first app to be localized this broadly. We have focused on languages spoken in regions with large illiterate populations that also have a growing adoption rate of low-end smartphones. In many of those fifty languages, there were few if any learning apps for literacy. Subsequently, we have had a number of other partners develop other apps amenable to localization.

As more apps cover more of the "app map," we want to be able to continually monitor how effective these apps are at helping those using them.

---

[15]United Nations. "The 17 Goals," n.d., accessed February 19, 2025, https://sdgs.un.org/goals.

One of the beauties of using apps for learning is that anonymous usage data, collected as a user engages with the app, flows back to the developer. We can collect data on when the child plays the app, for how long, and more specific information, like which parts of the app showed more errors and where users were successful, without revealing the identity of the user. This is invaluable because of what we learn about two main features that are vital in any learning app. First, the app must be engaging—children won't learn if they don't feel inspired to use the app. Second, the app must be effective—the game must teach or reinforce skills that lead to improving overall literacy skills. Learning apps must be both fun and effective.

Captured usage data along with special activities or games that assess particular skills embedded in the app experience help us understand if users are engaged and learning. The analyses allow us to understand which apps or sequence of apps will most help a particular population or individual child. Even more importantly, this information helps us understand which apps and/or parts of apps are most successful. Our aim is to optimize the ever-growing collection of apps to maximize learning impact. We also want to adapt to the needs of a changing population over time. This process creates a dynamic cycle of improvement. As long as we and our partners (app developers, NGOs, schools, ministries of education, etc.) remain curious and mine the data for what it can tell us, then all of us (Curious Learning, our partners, and the children) continue to learn. This unites us all as curious learners.

———

Back in the village, as we sat on the dirt floor with the women learning to read, they and their teacher finished their class. After asking a number of questions, the funder turned to us. As my colleague flipped through the textbooks and workbooks, I asked a few questions myself. How often were classes held? For how long? How well-attended were they? We were handed a notebook in which the teacher had been taking attendance. Flipping through it, we found that the class met three times a week, each session was about one-and-a-half hours, and we estimated that the women attended the classes about 50 percent of the time. A quick conversation with the teacher confirmed this. It also revealed that the low attendance was a byproduct of the many things in these women's lives that demanded their attention, like work, cooking, caring for children, illness—in other words, everything you need to do to ensure your family's survival when you live in a small rural village in India.

We quickly did the math.

Women in the village:

$$2 \text{ years of program} \times 50 \text{ weeks/year} \times 3 \text{ classes/week} \times$$
$$1.5 \text{ hours/class} \times 50 \text{ percent attendance} = 225 \text{ hours}$$

Children in school:

$$4 \text{ years of school} \times 8 \text{ months} \times 4.3 \text{ weeks/month} \times 5 \text{ days/week} \times$$
$$3 \text{ hours/day of reading instruction} = 2,064 \text{ hours}$$

Children learning to read have ten times (an order of magnitude) more exposure to learning. In addition, they are not burdened with the stresses and responsibilities of these women. By this measure of time on task, the women should have been expected to be at the same reading level as a child three months into kindergarten. From what we saw, they were well past that. Their brains had certainly started the process of being rewired to learn important reading skills.

What these women had achieved was remarkable.

I could see why the funder was concerned. These women had been at it for two years, and they were adults. To her mind, adults should be able to learn faster than children. She figured there must be something wrong with the program. The funder needed help realigning her expectations, understanding just how much work it is to learn to read and how hard it is to integrate that work into an adult's life. This was not the conversation she expected from us, but, to her credit, she engaged and became a curious learner.

In conversation with our host, we learned that more than half of the women had already learned their numbers and sufficient literacy skills to use a cellphone. So the men had to concede and allow them to have cellphones of their own. What was even more wonderful was that this new tool allowed them to find work more easily. As a result, family incomes greatly increased, in some cases as much as doubled.

We have to allow success to be reframed by those we are working to help. If we don't, we bring our own expectations and definitions of success to the table, thus imposing our own views and values upon them. Instead, we need to listen to those we wish to help, being attentive to what it is they need and what goals they aim to achieve. Failing to honor their aspirations, we disempower the very people we work so hard to lift up.

It is astounding how significant an impact even basic literacy skills can have on one's life, on the life of a family, and on an entire community.

During our long car ride north the next day, our conversation kept returning to the women in the village. What would have happened if they'd had smartphones at the beginning of their literacy journey, rather than receiving them later as a reward? They would have been able to use apps to aid their learning, and they could have used them at any time throughout the day or night, whenever and wherever they had a few free moments to play and learn. They would have been able to use their phones sooner to increase their income. How many more hours of practice and instruction would they have gotten over the two years? How much more progress would they have made? Would they have met the expectations of the funder then? Would their family income have more than doubled?

The Power of a
New Medium

Don't Blame the Medium,
Reframe the Message

We had spent months scouring the app store for apps appropriate for literacy learning, finding tablets to fill with these apps, and working with partners around the world to get them into the hands of kids who would otherwise never learn to read. We had research sites on four continents, in six countries (India, South Africa, Ethiopia, Uganda, Peru, and the United States), delivering all kinds of data and insights directly to us. Numerous insights about their effectiveness were coming into focus as we finished up our whirlwind tour of many of these sites and had analyzed our field notes and the large amounts of data we had collected.

We were desperate to find likeminded people who would be equally excited about our discoveries. We now had a true cross-cultural perspective on whether children around the world could learn to read from apps and also the kinds of apps kids were most likely to use, enjoy, and learn from. As exciting and compelling as this was, we had come to the conclusion that the apps already available only covered a fraction of the skills children needed to acquire to become competent readers. We needed to find allies who would be excited to develop new apps and to develop them in ways that could easily be adapted to a variety of languages.

In the fall of 2014, as a part of our search for allies, we were on our way to a small app developers conference that was specifically focused on educational apps. The conference took place in a small town on the Delaware river, meters from Washington's historic 1776 crossing, and included about one hundred attendees, people who were passionate about using apps to help children learn—the kindred spirits we'd been dreaming of. We had reached out to the organizer, and he was kind enough to invite us to speak. He had cultivated a community of people who were at the forefront of a new medium of touchscreens that were intuitive and natural for children to use, important qualities for helping them learn. We anticipated that these people would be receptive to our findings and excited to apply our insights to the app design and development process. We were ready to roll up our sleeves, share with them, and learn from them. Best of all, we wouldn't need to convince them or sell them on the promise of this new medium. This was going to be a fun and exciting few days. If it went well, we would return home with new friends who were excited to create new apps and who would help realize our ambition of using this powerful new medium to help everyone, globally, learn to read.

This little conference was definitely on the cutting edge. The first smartphones had only been on the market for six years. The first tablets were even newer. These new devices had a kind of magic about them. They were highly interactive and very intuitive. It was natural for anyone, including a small child, to reach out with their finger and touch the screen. The lack of a keyboard made the devices particularly accessible to young, preliterate children. There had been many efforts in the past to use computational devices to help children learn to read. But in many of those cases, one of the primary interfaces was the keyboard itself. It seems obvious now, but it took some trial and error for folks to understand that it's difficult for a child who doesn't even know their letters yet to use a keyboard as an interface.

These devices were so natural to use that we would just hand them out to the children at our research sites without even telling them how to turn them on. We would just sit back and observe how they explored the devices. Everywhere we went, at least one child would figure out within minutes how to turn it on. This knowledge would then spread like wildfire through the group. Ten minutes later, every child would have turned their device on. Uninhibited, they would explore on the screen by touching and dragging. Within weeks and with no special instruction, children were using the devices proficiently, navigating rapidly among apps and exploring how each app worked.

We had started to think of these devices not just as a new technology but as a totally new medium. Others in the field weren't quite there yet. A technology can empower a medium but does not fundamentally change the way you relate to the message. Take, for example, the written word. The printing press introduced a new technology that had a profound impact on who could access the written word; over time, it made the medium of the written word ubiquitous and widely available. These new devices go a step further by fundamentally changing the way people react to and interact with educational content, making them a new medium, not just a new technology. They do so across a variety of technologies, including laptops, smartphones, and tablets. Those attending the conference felt the same way. They were so excited about the possibilities, that they were investing their time, money, and careers in the development and design of apps for this medium, specifically to help children learn. They shared a passion and love for how this new medium could transform education and, more importantly, children's personal learning journeys. Needless to say, we were received by a friendly crowd.

———

Outside this circle, not everyone saw this new medium as positive. There had been a great deal of concern about children spending too much time in front of screens. Because these new devices were highly engaging and very attractive, they might become too compelling, maybe even addictive for children.

There was a strong and understandable concern that we should not introduce our children to new devices that would be harmful to them. A series of studies popped up trying to tease out the impact that time with these devices was having on children. What most of the studies illuminated was that a large amount of time on screens replaced time kids normally spent doing physical activities, such as participating in sports.[16] So, the byproduct of time spent on screens was a negative impact on the physical health of children.

These devices were relatively new, and they had only just begun to be integrated into families' lives. Most people were not seeing them as a new

---

[16]J. S. Radesky, J. Schumacher, and B. Zuckerman, "Mobile and Interactive Media Use by Young Children: The Good, the Bad, and the Unknown," *Pediatrics* 135, no. 1 (2015): 1–3. https://doi.org/10.1542/peds.2014-2251.

medium in and of themselves. Studies were overlooking the nuance that what you do on these devices might be an important part of determining their value. In other words, devices can be used in multiple ways, some considered positive and some negative. From this point of view, the device itself was not inherently good or bad.

Let's take, for example, television. For many years, TV was labeled the "boob tube," implying that the technology itself was negative. Over time, this point of view shifted—it became clear that the medium of TV could be used for a range of programming, from pornography to Sesame Street. The latter has become a cherished educational resource by parents and teachers alike. With any new medium, it takes time for us as a society to assess it, to explore how we can best use it and how and whether we as individuals want to bring it into our lives.[17] The unease surrounding new technologies goes all the way back to Socrates,[18] who was concerned about young people learning to write. He warned that being literate would be the downfall of the oral tradition and would weaken the mental powers of youth. There's no doubt that literacy did have an impact on society, in ways we now can't fully fathom. It is also true that the written word has allowed us to record and thereby share what we've learned, experienced, and created with many others, now and into the future.

Even if we choose not to think of this new technology as a new medium and harbor concerns about its use, it is now becoming quite clear that we cannot stop its widespread adoption. As of 2020, there were approximately 3.5 billion people in the world with smartphones.[19] That is about 45 percent of the entire population of the planet. This has been growing at a rate of 8 to 9 percent per year, reaching 6.8 billion people,

---

[17]A. Orben, "The Sisyphean Cycle of Technology Panics," *Perspectives on Psychological Science*, 15, no. 5 (2020): 1143–57. https://journals.sagepub.com/doi/10.1177/1745691620919372

[18]Plato. *Phaedrus and Letters VII and VIII*, trans. with introduction by Walter Hamilton (Penguin Books, 1973), pp. 274–7.

[19]Newzoo, "Number of Smartphone Users Worldwide from 2016 to 2021," In *Statista-The Statistics Portal*, September 2019, accessed February 17, 2021, https://www.statista.com/statistics/330695/number-of-smartphone-users-worldwide/#:~:text=The%20number%20of%20smartphone%20users,the%20100%20million%20user%20mark.

or 70 percent of global population, as of 2023.[20] As is often the case, new devices are first adopted in higher-income countries. Yet, as of 2023, in sub-Saharan Africa, 33 percent of people[21] had a smartphone in a region where only 12 percent of the population reads at grade level by the fourth grade.[22] With most homes having several adults in them, it is reasonable to think that over 50 percent of homes have access to a smartphone, even in the most impoverished countries. This number is only growing as prices drop and the benefits smartphones provide increase.

Communities in low-income countries are leapfrogging the technologies that most of us in high-income countries have had for decades and often continue to use. For example, their primary way of connecting to the Internet is via mobile data on a smartphone. Both the device and the bandwidth are cheaper and more accessible than laptops and cables, and the infrastructure to support it is much easier to deploy. In India, the cost of data is about nine cents per GB, versus US$8 per GB in the United States[23]—one hundred times cheaper. With the cost of low-end smartphones dropping below US$50, this puts them in the range of not more than one month of income for an adult in poverty making around US$2 per day. While this seems like a huge percentage of their annual income, the access to other work, resources, and information makes the expense worth it. This is particularly true in countries like Nepal where many families exist on remittances. One family member is often working outside the country and sending money back home. In this case, they also often bring back or purchase a smartphone for their family at home, and

---

[20]What's the Big Data, "How Many People Own Smartphones? (2024–2029)," https://whatsthebigdata.com/smartphone-stats/.

[21]GSMA Intelligence, "The Mobile Economy Sub-Saharan Africa 2020," 2020, https://www.gsmaintelligence.com/research/the-mobile-economy-sub-saharan -africa-2020, estimated 25% of adults in SSA already had a smartphone. www .statista.com shows that in 2022 there were 415 million (estimated to grow to 689 million by 2028) smartphones subscriptions in SSA, so with a population of 1.24 billion that is over 33 percent as of 2023.

[22]United Nations Statistics Division, "Sustainable Development Goals Report," 2019, accessed February 17, 2021, https://unstats.un.org/sdgs/report/2019 /Overview/.

[23]Cable.co.uk, "Worldwide Mobile Data Pricing 2020: The Cost of 1GB of Mobile Data in 228 Countries," February 2020, accessed February 17, 2021, https://www.cable.co.uk/mobiles/worldwide-data-pricing/.

the phone becomes the primary means of maintaining a connection to the family.

Even in the spring of 2020, with the pandemic hitting, we were being asked by people just learning about our work whether or not parents with low income would allow their children to use their smartphones. In their minds, a smartphone was such a precious device, these parents might not want their children using it for fear they might break it. Our experience does not support this notion. In 2018, a partner of ours in Nairobi performed a test where a facilitator espoused the value of literacy learning apps that parents could load onto their smartphones during their school's parent–teacher conference. Eighty percent of those with a phone installed the app; two weeks later, 75 percent of them had allowed their kids to use it extensively. In northern Nigeria, in 2019, the World Bank ran a test where smartphones preloaded with Feed the Monster and the Global Digital Library were distributed to homes. At the end of the study period, it was found that not only were two-thirds of the children reading books, but their parents also reported being more motivated to send their daughters to school after seeing how well they learned.

My informal conversations with parents in impoverished communities often go like this: I ask them if they allow their children to use their smartphones; they, often reluctantly, admit that they do and that their children (like children everywhere) are always bugging them to use their phones to play games. The parents are often concerned that it is not good for their kids to play games (like Candy Crush). I then ask, "If you had a game that would help your children learn, would you let them use the phone to play it?" They always respond with an emphatic "Yes" and then they ask how they can acquire these games so their kids can begin using them right away.

Even with the growing reach and the inevitable proliferation of these devices, we still often meet resistance to this new medium when talking to leaders in the ministries of education of various countries. Ministries of education are used to reaching 100 percent of their population, or at least feeling like they are reaching 100 percent. When they adopt an educational material or process, they implement this change in all of their schools. By doing so, this approach is seen as reaching all students and is supposed to be available to everyone. When a solution is introduced to them that requires mobile phones, they may only be able to reach 50 percent of the homes, as of 2020. In their minds, that is unacceptable—it must be available to 100 percent of the population or to no one.

Even when governments believe they are reaching 100 percent of children, that notion tends to be a farce. Not all children even attend school regularly, and very few of them are learning. In many impoverished schools, both teacher and student attendance rates contribute to only about two-thirds of the scheduled school time being available to learning.[24] On top of that, in sub-Saharan Africa, only 12 percent of children are reading at grade level by fourth grade.[25] So, clearly, the existing approach, while reaching a supposed "100 percent" of students, is actually only meeting ministry goals for about 12 percent of the population. It is like saying we are not going to teach anyone how to read until everyone can afford a pencil, paper, and a book. But the reality is that people rarely need a pencil, paper, or a book until they can already read.

Mobile devices and educational apps are unique in a few important ways. This is not just a medium for delivering educational content, but it is also a technology that can measure the impact of this method of learning on its users. THIS IS A BIG DEAL. It would be like having a textbook that could send you (the teacher, parent, textbook author) a message that a child has read the chapter and answered the questions. It could also let you know which answers they got right and which ones wrong. This textbook could even talk to its reader, saying, "It looks like you missed concept X in the previous chapter, so I am going to review that with you." The textbook could send messages to both educators and authors so they could better assess what's working and what's not, allowing them to push out changes to the "textbook" in real time and immediately see if and how those changes improve the learning process. This has never been possible

---

[24]One study I looked at did some calculations on teacher absenteeism, learner absenteeism, and time on and off learning in school. It found that just barely two-thirds of time in school (two-and-a-half hours) for just 6 months per year (because either the teacher or the child is absent for some part of the other 3 months of the school year) is spent actually learning. (E. Friedlander, "The Untapped Learning Potential of the Home and Community in the Developing World," NIAS Conference on Global Literacy, Nijmegen, Holland, March 2016.)

[25]See United Nations, "Sustainable Development Goals Report."

before, but it does parallel what our best teachers do on a small scale every day in their classrooms. Imagine how empowered teachers would be with these tools. And how those teachers who lack certain skills could themselves learn how they might more deeply participate in the learning process of their students.

Every three years, countries all around the world administer a test to their fifteen-year-olds called the Programme for International Student Assessment (PISA). In addition to assessing math, reading, and science skills, the test asks other questions of students and teachers. The 2018 PISA included questions about the use of technology. A McKinsey report (McKinsey & Company) used this data to better understand how technology affects learning in the classroom. The report's first chart showed that the use of Internet-connected computers that were connected to projectors, allowing everyone to share the same screen, was associated with higher student outcomes, while the use of tablets by individuals was associated with lower student outcomes. The report had nothing to say about how these technologies were being used. In the introduction, the report admits that it cannot "answer questions on the eventual potential of education technology—but it can powerfully tell us the extent to which that potential is being realized today in classrooms around the world."

Despite McKinsey's admission of the limited scope of its report, many organizations hold it up as a condemnation of the use of certain technologies in education. In other words, the report is interpreted as providing supporting evidence that technology, such as tablets, should not be used in classrooms—or only used under certain circumstances. This is a clear example of seeing this new technology as just that, an object that you simply turn on or off, instead of as a new medium with great potential that we are still learning how to use for the benefit of our students.

———

Back at the conference, we were with fellow pioneers at the forefront of what was (and still is) possible. We started our talk with an overview of the research we had been doing around the world and quickly moved to what everyone was most excited about—what kinds of apps were needed and what kind of app design was most effective. We reported on design issues, such as the fact that most young children have a strong preference for apps that let them start interacting right away. For example, when an app started with a longer monologue from an animated character explaining what they would be doing, kids quickly left that app in search of something else.

The data also reminded us of just how hard it is for literate adults to anticipate what will engage a young beginning reader, even adults who are design professionals. There was one app that we were even hesitant to include in our research. The app, Alphabet Blocks, was simple. All twenty-six letters would appear on the screen, each in its own square. When a child touched a letter, it became animated and a voice would say the name of the letter, vocalize its sound, and offer a word beginning with it. The object or animal whose name began with the letter became animated. The app's graphics were fairly basic, certainly not up to the standard to which this audience was accustomed. Nevertheless, user data showed that the app was highly engaging and impactful for children of a certain level of development and learning. Kids would spend hours playing with it and repeating what was being said. And to think, we nearly left this app out of the study altogether.

The conference audience was highly engaged. We had provided a wealth of information to help them improve the products they were creating, and we had outlined the new products that were needed and possible. There were several points in the presentation where audience members raised their phones to take pictures of the slides on the screen for later reference. We were very excited to connect with a likeminded crowd. During the Q and A, we were asked what kinds of devices the children were using and, more specifically, what apps they were using. For the most part, we had used the low-end tablets of the time. They were slower and were not as well-designed as high-end devices, but they were sufficient and economical. As we showed some of the apps that people in the audience were less familiar with, we could feel the audience shift.

As we left the stage, the person who was introducing the next speaker approached us and gave voice to the shift we'd sensed. He felt that children everywhere desired "the best." In his and likely others' minds, "the best" meant a high-end iPad and the kinds of high-end apps that most of the developers in the audience were creating. They were all coming from a genuine interest in helping children. They wanted children all over the world to have what they felt was best. They were excited about what wonderful products they could design and build, and they wanted to share those with the world. While they had embraced this technology as a new medium well before others had, they had missed one of the most important elements of a medium. A medium can be used many different ways by many different people. Their idea of "the best" was not necessarily best for everyone. Our data showed that it was not what a six-year-old living in the slums of Kampala thought was best. Without even realizing it, they had fallen into the same trap people throughout history have fallen into—assuming they knew what was best for someone else. Even with the best of intentions, it is easy to fall into this kind of trap, one we need to be diligent in avoiding.

———

Even as recently as fall of 2019, we found ourselves sitting at a table with people from large multilaterals and ministries of education, bumping our heads against concerns about using smartphones for early education. But sometimes events conspire to help us look at things in a different light, help us reconsider or even abandon previous beliefs. In the spring of 2020, the pandemic hit and schools all over the world closed. While this by no means removed all the barriers to the use of smartphones for literacy learning, it did start shifting beliefs. People now saw smartphones as one of the best tools for continuing education, in particular in low-income countries, and one of the only practical ways to reach younger children who were not in school. Our conversation partners were now ready to discuss how best to use this medium. In short, the pandemic catalyzed new ways for us to think about education. For those working with this new medium, more doors were opening than closing.

It takes time to understand a new medium and how it can be used for the betterment of society. We have to remain open, allowing ourselves and others to experiment. Then we have to step back and find objective ways to understand its impact. Just as importantly, we need to step outside the boxes of our current beliefs with a willingness to examine whether those beliefs still hold value or whether they, instead, limit ideas of what is possible.

Interestingly, we have been working hard, finding ways to use the medium of touchscreens to help children learn to read; the need for reading is a product of the advent of the written word—the very thing that concerned Socrates. Today, the skills of reading and writing are central to our society; we now classify them as basic human rights. The world changes and evolves. I don't think we would want it any other way, which is a good thing, because we couldn't stop it if we tried.

Curriculum Conundrum

Fear of Change Is an Indicator of a Limiting Belief That Needs to Change

It was the winter of 2014 in South Africa. We had just left Durban and were driving up the coast of KwaZulu-Natal with the ocean in the distance to the east and sugarcane fields to the west. We were on our way to a government school about halfway to the border of Mozambique. We wanted to determine whether tablets and apps could help the students there learn to read.

As we reached the edge of a long stretch of sugarcane fields, we saw housing scattered across the hillside. Much of it was built by the inhabitants from whatever materials they could gather. Corrugated metal is often used as a building material in these informal settlements. Our hosts explained that many of the parents whose kids went to the school worked in the sugarcane fields as laborers. The housing we had noticed on the edge of the fields was where many of them lived.

We turned off the main road and headed a short distance up a side road before leaving the pavement to turn toward a gate. Our host waved and someone opened the gate for us. We pulled into a dirt courtyard where we parked between a handful of buildings with open windows. At the far end of the parking lot-courtyard-playground sat a series of additional buildings that looked temporary. I asked about them and was told they had been set up to handle the burgeoning overflow of students. Previously, classes had been held under the trees. Close to 800 students were enrolled in the school in about eight different grade levels. The class sizes ranged from fifty to one hundred kids per classroom, with only one teacher. It already felt like those temporary buildings were relegated to becoming permanent.

We started to walk around while getting a quick tour. We had planned to spend the better part of the next week there, observing the school's operations and the reading levels of the children. We found that we needed to spend at least a few days just hanging out before the novelty of our presence wore off and teachers and students alike fell back into their normal patterns and behaviors. This was the only way we could gain a deeper understanding of what was going on.

The buildings were simple cinder block structures with windows on both sides and flat metal roofs. The windows were left wide open to capture what little cross-ventilation was available. In the courtyard was a tank of water and a spigot, but there were no bathrooms or sinks. Behind the buildings were latrines, open cesspits. I watched as a kid came around a building and walked up to an ingenious contraption: a recycled plastic jug hung from a post; a string was tied to the jug and to a makeshift pedal on the ground. When the kid placed his foot on the pedal, the jug tipped, and water poured out over his waiting hands and onto the ground. There were a number of these scattered around the play yard that were periodically refilled from the spigot.

Our host and partner was a representative from Mr. Price Foundation, a South Africa–based nonprofit that seeks to improve children's education. Mr. Price Foundation chose to work with this school in an effort to provide them with additional resources. Over time, this included capital improvements, but they started their support by looking at what kinds of technologies could help the educational process.

The students, teachers, and staff were happy, engaged, and very welcoming. Teachers and school personnel were all enthusiastically interested in helping these children learn. Despite so much support, these children, like many across South Africa, would struggle to become proficient readers. We needed several years, multiple visits, conversations, and research to understand at least some of the reasons for this. One reason that was immediately apparent, though, was that class sizes were enormous. Even the most skilled teacher would find it difficult to teach to a classroom of seventy-five-plus students.

This school was in better shape than many. Not only were the teachers and staff highly motivated, but they had more knowledge than the average teacher. Despite that, they, like most teachers in South Africa, had received little training in the specifics of reading instruction and were often locked into a rigid, state-mandated curriculum. With such large classroom sizes and the need to keep order, the majority of the teaching process involved the children repeating the material from the curriculum in a call-and-response interaction. Over the course of a year, there were approximately 140 school days and forty days' worth of other self-guided activities, like worksheets and other exercises.

Poor learning outcomes were further exacerbated by erratic attendance. On any given day, 50 to 60 percent of students were absent. There were many reasons for this widespread problem. Many students walked to school; during times of adverse weather, they often stayed at home. Older siblings were required to stay home and help care for sick relatives. At the time of our visit, rarely a week went by when there was not a funeral for someone in the community who had passed away from HIV/AIDS.

As if these challenges were not enough, the language of instruction posed one of the most complex issues. When apartheid fell in South Africa, long and extensive discussions and negotiations were held to decide which languages would become official national languages. As language is so intertwined with culture and identity, many groups understandably wanted their languages represented. The decision was made to adopt eleven South African languages to hold official status, which paved the way for the right of parents to choose the language of instruction for their children. At first glance, this would seem like a great idea that not only supports language development and cultural preservation but allows children to learn in their mother tongue. The research is clear on the importance of learning to read in one's first language.[26] Those skills can then be used to learn to speak and read other languages.

But here's the rub: In this school, children up to the end of the third grade learned to read in isiZulu. Suddenly, at the fourth grade, instruction switched over to English, as it did nationwide. Again, this seemed like a good idea, as there was very little educational material in the other ten languages, and it moved children to a global language, creating better employment opportunities.

---

[26]A. C. Izuagba and A. O. Afurobi, "Developing Teachers' Capacity for Teaching Pupils' Initial Reading Skills: Research Report," *African Research Review* 10 no. 4 (2016): 93–105. https://doi.org/10.4314/afrrev.v10i4.7.

So, this all seemed well and fine on paper. Unfortunately, in practice, there was little to no support as a child moved into fourth grade and was instantly thrown into an environment using a new language they didn't necessarily speak and certainly hadn't mastered. So, with the lack of support to learn English, nonnative English speakers fell desperately behind. As a result, some students stopped attending school. Those who stayed in school got some benefit, including food and socialization, but often moved through the grades without mastering the material. Imagine the disorientation of being thrown into a fourth-grade classroom where the teacher spoke a language you didn't know, while your whole life outside of the classroom continued in your mother tongue.

Years later, after our first visit to the school, this issue played out on a larger scale. In 2017, South Africa adopted a policy that gave everyone the opportunity to attend university—free higher education for all. Again, a noble and ambitious idea. Students matriculated from their secondary education with excitement to take advantage of this new opportunity. Once at university, they quickly found themselves unable to keep up with the work. Students and parents started protesting against the government for not having adequately prepared students for university. They felt cheated and deceived; they had no way of knowing how inadequate their education had been.

After our tour and the opportunity to observe some of the classrooms, we sat down with staff at the end of the school day to plan how the tablets we had brought them would be used in the classroom. Our partner had acquired enough tablets to provide an entire classroom of students with their own tablets. They also provisioned the tablets with the apps we provided. A big part of the discussion revolved around deciding which kids would be given access to the tablets, how often, and under what conditions. As the discussion progressed, it became clear that one of the primary concerns was whether the use of the tablets would comply with the state-mandated curriculum. As in many countries, the South African Ministry of Education hands down strict requirements about exactly how many hours of instruction must be devoted to each subject for each grade level throughout the day. The teachers and the school must track these hours, and they risk being sacked if deemed noncompliant. No matter how excited the teachers were to bring the tablets into the classroom, without the reassurance that time spent with the tablet would count toward curriculum hours, they were understandably concerned.

This was only the first of many similar discussions we would have with educators around the world. Any new or supplemental approach faces constant pressure to be heavily curriculum-aligned. The demands to comply are rooted in the history and tradition of curriculum development and deployment. Traditionally, curricula have been disseminated through printed materials, like books and workbooks, which are expensive to produce and demand an enormous amount of time to develop and share. So the traditional method of developing a curriculum was to pour over it for years with experts and ministers, making sure everything was acceptable and vetted by as many of the stakeholders as possible. Once approved, the materials were produced and disseminated knowing there would be no opportunity to amend, adapt, or revise them for decades to come. For a long time, even in high-income countries, there was little or no research done to assess how effective any curriculum was at reaching educational goals. The long lead times and the large costs involved in changing a curriculum removed the political will to analyze whether or not it was working. Only in recent decades have educational impact studies become part of the practice of curriculum development, but, even now, this is not the norm. In low-income countries or former colonies, most curricula and teaching methods are based upon the structures adopted decades ago from colonial cultures and schools; no tradition of curriculum evaluation arrived as a part of those adopted methods.

In South Africa and throughout sub-Saharan Africa, these curricula are not working.

Seventy-eight percent of South African children cannot read for meaning in the fourth grade.[27] That number is closer to 88 percent across the rest of sub-Saharan Africa. The colonial curriculum that produces these abysmal results has become so much a part of the social norm that any mention of changing the curriculum may be perceived as a broader attack on the culture, which is ironic considering these curricula were a

---

[27]I. V. S. Mullis, M. O. Martin, P. Foy, and M. Hooper, *PIRLS 2016 International Results in Reading* (International Association for the Evaluation of Educational Achievement [IEA], 2017).

colonial imposition. Preserving an alignment with the norms of society, represented in this case by the curriculum, holds the highest value, even when these norms do not produce desirable results.

Is there a way to "decolonize" a curriculum? A way to support the development and alteration of the curriculum so that it meets the needs of society by giving children the ability to learn to read while also embodying and being respectful of the local culture and language?

In the spirit of experimentation, we decided to make the tablets available to kids during certain "free times" throughout the week, meaning during the rare few hours that were not curriculum-mandated. Certain classrooms would have the opportunity to use the tablets two or three times a week for approximately forty-five minutes each time. This solution also greatly increased the amount of time children had to actively engage with educational activities. There is power in using a technology-based medium for the delivery of educational content. It means you can try things rapidly and quickly collect data. Usage data, like time spent, number of touches, and what was touched, can demonstrate engagement; assessment data can show if educational goals are being supported and at what rate. All this can be done over the course of weeks. This is not the way the educational system generally thinks and works. We had found collaborators in just such an experiment and a way to test this approach without impinging on curriculum demands.

We came back the next day, the first day of the experiment. We passed out the tablets, and we did not tell the children how to turn them on. These kids were so used to sitting and following orders that they quietly stared at us and the teachers without touching the tablets. It was not until a few kids felt like they were not being watched that they started to experiment and figure out how to turn their tablets on. Once the first kid realized that this behavior was not going to be punished, their neighbors followed, starting a chain reaction; within ten minutes, all the children were experimenting with one of the apps.

We wanted to see how the children would do with the tablets without instructions, so we asked the teachers not to explain anything to them. This was very difficult for the teachers, whose impulse was to assist the children, especially those who seemed to be struggling. With some reminding, the teachers managed to wait and watch. With the children fully engaged with the tablets, the classroom was very focused and quiet. This created a rare experience for the teachers, where they did not need to be in charge or exert control. It allowed them to walk the classroom and observe, so they could better understand what was on the tablets and how they were being used by the children. At the end of the school day, the teachers were so excited to share their experiences and how surprised they were. One teacher remarked, "I had no idea that boy knew so much. He is always so quiet."

Over the years since 2014, we would return to this school and other isiZulu-speaking communities. During one of these visits, we brought Feed the Monster, which we had localized into isiZulu. Feed the Monster helps kids identify the sounds letters make and how to blend these sounds together to make words. Once a child has learned the letter sounds, they have the skills needed to begin to sound out words. Many of us may remember this process from our own education or our children's. But after spending many days in the classrooms watching how the children were taught to read in isiZulu, my colleague made a simple but extremely astute observation: We had found a better way to teach reading in isiZulu.

IsiZulu is an agglutinative language, which means it strings together a number of syllables to make words and full sentences. Most words can get quite long and complicated to spell. An extreme example of this is the isiZulu word for the number eight: *ayisishiyagalombili.* Imagine that you are learning to read isiZulu and have just spent time mastering the sounds of the twenty-six letters. Now, you're given *ayisishiyagalombili* to sound out. It is no wonder children were hitting a wall in learning to read at this point. Being a linguist, my colleague studied the local research on the knowledge of fluent adult readers in isiZulu. What was common among skilled readers was the automaticity with which they could read forty to fifty common syllables. We made a simple adjustment to the app; instead of moving from letter sounds straight to words, we created an intermediate step, where the children could learn these fifty basic syllables before moving on to trying to read words. Now, these long, daunting words would no longer look like a massive string of letters that were hard to parse. The kids would actually be able to see the syllables.

One small but simple step toward "decolonizing" a curriculum.

As we returned repeatedly over the years to observe the kids and meet with our partners, several unintended consequences emerged. The first was that, within months of beginning to use the tablets, the school reported that their absentee rate had dropped significantly! Kids were much more interested in coming to school, rain or shine. This was particularly true on the days when they were going to be using the apps. The children enjoyed using these apps so much that they did not want to miss days when it was their turn.

Word spread through the larger communities to parents of students at adjacent schools. The perception was that this school was doing great things, creating great opportunities for learning. Parents started moving their children to this school. Over the course of a few years, the school saw its enrollment rise by at least 50 percent—from around 800 children to over 1,200. Enrollment at neighboring schools declined. We were thrilled that the program was so well-received by both children and parents, but we could never have anticipated this level of enthusiasm. Unfortunately, new pressures were placed on the school. Their already large classroom sizes were now pushed even further. By this time, we were already moving away from pilot studies that involved managing tablets in schools. We were starting to focus on making sure the apps could be used on low-end smartphones that more and more parents were acquiring. Was this a way to make sure that any parent could make this resource available to their child without the need to switch schools? For the schools, was it a way to make this available to their students without the expense and logistics of acquiring and managing equipment?

One of the more unexpected and pleasant surprises was what happened with the teachers. The teachers' curiosity was piqued to the point that they spent a lot of time watching the kids play with the apps, and even played with the apps themselves. This gave them new insights not only into how the kids were learning but also into how the apps were instructing the children. This led them to changing their teaching styles. In the same way that children's curiosity drove their learning, teachers' curiosity drove their own learning that helped them grow as teachers. The apps had become a learning tool for both the students and the teachers!

This had been an experiment to see if these apps would help children learn to read. They ended up doing far more than that. By leaving both the children and the teachers to explore for themselves, we had unknowingly shifted their mindset. This started with us not even telling the children how to turn the tablets on. Allowing them to experiment unobserved empowered both the children and the teachers as learners. The whole process became what they wanted and what worked for them. By opening up space in the educational process for exploration, by moving teachers and students out of their lockstep curriculum, their energy for teaching and learning was reignited and elevated. All we had done was to offer them a few tools and invite them to do something for themselves, and this resulted in an inspiring demonstration of the power of enabling agency.

This transformation was an organic evolution of a curriculum powered by curiosity.

Experimentation powered by curiosity: Isn't that a good definition of learning? Or a definition that we aspire to? Isn't that what we are asking of our children? That they become curious, excited, and engaged learners? Don't we wish for them to experiment and realize that not getting something "right" is not a failure but an opportunity, a necessary step in the learning process? Throughout life, we learn by trying things, then modifying our behavior, then trying again. How can we as teachers and educators ask this of our children and not be willing to do it for ourselves? New ways of delivering learning experiences powered by ubiquitous technology afford us the opportunity to redefine how a curriculum is developed and is adapted over time. This is an opportunity to redefine what we mean by curriculum in a way that empowers everyone: the app developer, the school system, the teacher, the parents, and, most importantly, the children. All can play an important role in how we educate our children.

Illiteracy Is Never an Emergency

Moving from Surviving to Thriving

We were walking along a trail that locals would have called a road. Our 4x4 had been struggling on this so-called road, so we had decided to abandon it. I had stopped to take a picture, and by the time I looked up from my camera, Stephanie, who was about a hundred yards ahead of me, was barely visible in the mist. We were walking through a cloud at about 10,000 feet above sea level, which was like walking through air made of water droplets rather than beneath a light rain dropping down from above. As we walked for another mile, we passed a group of women on their way to town with objects balanced on their heads. They emerged out of the mist, then disappeared back into it as they passed us, like mythical creatures that left us wondering whether or not we'd actually seen them. It was market day. Occasionally a burro with a sack or two of grain strapped to its back would pass, more often than not, unaccompanied. Our guides explained that the burros were so accustomed to walking between the village and the town that they were often left to finish the journey on their own.

As the mist lifted, and the sun started to peek from between the clouds, the cool, damp air warmed and dried. Looking down from one side of the trail, we saw a beautiful clear blue mountain lake nestled in the steep slopes. On the other side, we could see our destination, the village, which consisted of a series of thatched roofs. Among them, an old man stood in the distance holding an umbrella over his head. While the umbrella wasn't in the best of shape, it clearly was a prized possession—few if anyone in the village had anything like it. I suspected the man used it rain or shine, as protection from both sun and rain. Just as we started down toward the village, several young kids came running up the hillside to greet us.

We were in Ethiopia, visiting one of the two original villages in the research study that began in 2012. The village, situated somewhere between 10,000 and 11,000 feet, was lush and green and hosted an agrarian lifestyle. Villagers grew crops for their own consumption as well as for selling and trading at a market a two-hour walk away. Since there was no accessible school, there was no expectation that the children in this village would attend school. No one in the village was literate in the local language of Oromo. No one spoke English, although English was an aspirational language here as all schooling after the fourth grade was in English. All the apps on the tablets had been chosen to help the children learn some basic English vocabulary and learn to read in English. At the time, there were no educational apps in Oromo, so an English aspirational community had been chosen.

One hut was set up with solar panels on the roof and provided a place to charge the tablets. While the material and equipment had been provided, the community had worked together to build and set up the hut for the children's use. It had been two years since they were first given the tablets. After one year with the tablets, their early reading skills had been assessed. Much to our surprise, the majority of the twenty-plus children had reached roughly the same level of basic literacy skills typically achieved in a well-resourced U.S. kindergarten. These were the results that inspired the founding of Curious Learning and inspired others to start working in this space.[28]

On this trip back to the village, our plan was to check on the kids' progress once again. After a brief walk around the village, it started to rain, so we retreated to a hut with the children and a few adults. Sitting on simple benches and scattered bags of grain, we started the process of assessing the kids' reading skills. As the rain turned to hail and grew increasingly louder, it became difficult to hear one another. This provided a natural break, which allowed us space for conversations with some of the adults in the village, with the help of a translator. While life in the village seemed very physically demanding, people seemed quite happy and very excited for the opportunity for their children to learn from the tablets.

---

[28]In particular, the XPRIZE, https://www.xprize.org/prizes/global-learning. We supported XPRIZE as consultants and judges.

They had a deep sense of pride for what their children had accomplished. The children themselves were highly engaged and had started talking about the kinds of careers or opportunities they might like to pursue. One young girl talked of becoming a doctor and bringing those skills back to her village. Another boy was inspired by the small team we had partnered with to provide the tablets and set up the solar panels. He expressed an interest in working with technology. This certainly seemed like a village that was not just surviving but was thriving. The tablets seemed to be providing a tool that expanded that thriving.

A day or two later, we visited the second village, but under very different circumstances. Again, we had to abandon the four-wheel-drive vehicle and walk the balance of the way to the village. This time, the soil was dry and there were numerous rocks in the way. We were in a desert out in the bush. No lush, green grass, just lots of dry dirt and sand. As we approached the village, we could see camels being led in the distance. Though there were no camels in the village, as no one in the village had the means to own one, they were commonly used by locals. Again, as we approached the village, we were greeted by children who ran to meet us. This time, they kicked up dust as they ran. The huts were of similar construction, with dirt floors and thatched roofs, but, here, many of the huts were surrounded by piles of a thorny bush used as a kind of fence. We learned from our guide that this helped keep some of the large wild cats from getting to both children and livestock. In this village, women and children walked ten kilometers each way, every day to gather water. In spite of how precious this water was to them, they held up bottles of brown liquid to share with us. We thanked them graciously but showed them that we had our own water.

We sensed that the dynamic or social structure in this village was very different from the first village. Men and women were strongly divided in this village. The women seemed to do most of the work, including gathering the water. Some of the men were partially blind from consuming alcohol they had made themselves. One young girl, who must have been no more than fourteen and who had been one of our star pupils a year earlier, was now pregnant and married. This village was definitely working hard just to survive. Despite these challenges, the kids were highly engaged with the educational apps.

Stephanie and I split up, hoping that she could get a better handle on what was going on with the women and girls in the village. The boys had been dominating the interactions with us. I stayed with the boys as she wandered off with the women and girls. After engaging with the boys for a while, I walked to the edge of the village. The boys headed off to other activities. A girl, maybe eight or nine years old, surprised me as she emerged from the bush wearing one shoe and a tattered jean jacket. As I turned to greet her, I pointed to myself and said my name, then pointed at her shoulder. She said, "Jacket," in English. Not believing what I'd heard, I repeated the gesture. Sure enough, again, she said, "Jacket." I picked up a stick and started to write letters in the dust and then words that I knew she could have learned from working with the apps on the tablets. One by one, she read them all. I hoped she would continue to learn rather than ending up pregnant and married in a few short years.

———

While visiting these two villages, I couldn't help but ponder the many big issues we wrestle with globally, from food insecurity to child labor to human trafficking to health and hygiene disparities. The more we dig and the more we learn, the more it seems the ability to read is integrally tied to our ability to transcend these other issues.

- Health: With literacy, people are five times more likely to know how HIV/AIDS is spread.
- Economic equality: Each grade level of literacy increases earnings by 9.7 percent.
- Food security: Literacy would increase food production by 24 percent.
- Human trafficking: Forty-six percent of Nigerian youth identify illiteracy as a major cause of human trafficking.
- Child labor: Forty-seven percent of child laborers will never attend school.
- Gender inequality: Two-thirds of illiterate adults are women.
- Peace: Without literacy, people are nine times more likely to become radicalized.

- Social Justice: Eighty percent of those incarcerated cannot read; 80 percent of juvenile offenders are functionally illiterate.
- Poverty: Basic literacy for 170 million illiterate adults would translate to a 12 percent reduction in world poverty.

A number of international aid programs illustrate the power of literacy skills to promote the long-term success of aid efforts. Aid programs also recognize that lack of literacy can limit desired aid outcomes. Ebola is an example of the limiting aspect of illiteracy. When the disease broke out in West Africa between 2014 and 2016, one of the most difficult tasks was educating people about its spread and how to prevent it. This task was made substantially more difficult because the majority of people health teams needed to reach were illiterate.

Another example of the limits of aid programs in areas of low literacy is found in the cocoa supply chain, which is riddled with child labor problems. The International Cocoa Initiative (ICI), a nonprofit organization, works closely with the cocoa and chocolate industries to eliminate child labor. As effective as some of these programs can be, ICI has learned that as soon as they stop running their programs, children are pulled back to the fields: The problem had not been sustainably solved. Members of the ICI recognize that it is not enough to reduce child labor practices or even draw attention to them. Communities affected by child labor need to be empowered to maintain a new social norm; education is the way to do that. Education not only opens doors to new opportunities, but it also leads the way to new beliefs about what is possible for children, farmers, and communities as a whole. Even a basic level of literacy can start to shift long-held beliefs. Literate children better understand how to protect themselves. Literate parents and farmers can envision better alternatives to child labor, as they themselves are less likely to be exploited. Improving literacy skills may not be the quick fix we would all hope for, but long-term systemic change will require that communities have at least a basic level of literacy.

Nutritional health is another area where increasing literacy would have an enormous impact. A number of research grants have been offered over the years to study nutritional interventions for populations that are effectively starving. While many of these programs have been highly effective at elevating the nutritional health of the populations they reach, they've learned that these programs are not sticky. As soon as the programs stop running at full force, there's no knowledge or wherewithal within communities to maintain their own nutritional health. Many granters are starting to require that these programs also run educational components. But the extent to which you can educate a population about their own health and nutrition is limited when they are not literate, as is the ability of those people to seek and acquire the nutritious foods that will help them maintain good health.

Another heartbreaking example of literacy's value: Years ago, a friend of mine was interviewing sex workers in Bangkok as research for a documentary film. One woman explained to him that she had arrived in Bangkok as a child after escaping a violent situation. She wandered the city until she was picked up and was forced to work as a child prostitute. She broke down in tears as she explained that if she had been able to read street signs as a child, she would have better understood where she was and what she was getting pulled into. If she had been able to read, she would have had a chance to make a choice, to find a better life for herself.

Literacy matters—that is clear. But we have only recently begun to recognize education as a human right. The 17 UN SDGs were adopted in 2015. Goal Number 4 is to "ensure inclusive and equitable quality education and promote lifelong learning opportunities for all." Literacy is a foundational skill for almost all education, so we can think of literacy as a human right. Everyone should be given the opportunity to learn to read. Just as everyone is entitled to food, clothing, and shelter, all people are entitled to the opportunity to learn to read.

In 2020, the pandemic hit, and the world went from about 200 million kids being out of school to over 1.5 billion kids out of school in a matter of weeks. Prior to the pandemic, it was estimated by the UNESCO Institute for Statistics that there were 773 million completely illiterate adults in the world.[29] If all of these adults could read at a first-grade level, global

---

[29]UIS (UNESCO Institute for Statistics), "Literacy", 2020, https://uis.unesco.org/en/topic/literacy

GDP would increase by US$1.2 trillion per year.[30] It has been estimated that the amount of educational loss due to the pandemic would equate to US$17 trillion[31] of lost income to those who missed out on educational opportunities. That's roughly US$22,000 over the course of a lifetime for every person affected. Now, the educational emergency has shifted from, "How can we make sure everyone has the basic human right to quality education?" to "How do we prevent backsliding by decades?"

Understandably, governments responded to the pandemic first by asking how they could keep people safe. Toward that end, the first tool was to close schools, removing them as vectors of transmission. Because of our work at Curious Learning, we were quickly pulled into conversations with a number of ministries of education and multilateral organizations. Most of these conversations focused on what could be done in lower-income countries. Technology and remote learning held the promise of continuing education while school closures were necessary. But in practice, it was difficult to reach everyone equitably, even in well-resourced countries. In low-income countries, it was even more difficult. Most solutions relied upon people having access to higher-end devices, like laptops and high-bandwidth Internet connections. Even where those were in place, teachers had to quickly figure out how to teach effectively over this new medium.

Overwhelmed and under-resourced, most of the ministries of education in low- and middle-income countries needed to triage the situation. They focused on children who were approaching their national testing grades, which is typically fourth grade or matriculation at tenth or twelfth grade. These countries faced an emergency situation, and they did not have the time or luxury to think about the repercussions of their actions four or five years down the road. Making sure that younger children would continue to learn to read was more than they were capable of taking on at that point. Continuing literacy learning did not cross the threshold of being included as an emergency action. While this charge to

---

[30] A. Cree, A. Kay, and J. Steward, "The Economic and Social Cost of Illiteracy: A Snapshot of Illiteracy in a Global Context," Final Report from the World Literacy Foundation, September 2022, https://worldliteracyfoundation.org/wp-content/uploads/2022/08/The-Economic-Social-Cost-of-Illiteracy-2022.pdf.

[31] The World Bank, UNESCO, and UNICEF, *The State of the Global Education Crisis: A Path to Recovery* (The World Bank, UNESCO, and UNICEF, 2021).

triage and focus on life-threatening issues over long-term needs was particularly relevant during the pandemic, in reality, it was there before the pandemic and will continue afterward for those in poverty.

Threats to life are particularly prevalent for those who dwell in poverty. Examples are not having enough to eat; not having access to basic health care (more specifically, wrestling with a life-threatening illness that is running through your community, like COVID, Ebola, or AIDS); being exploited; living in a war-torn environment; losing your home as a refugee. All these situations capture our attention, as they should. Emergency funding flows to them, and philanthropic resources end up focusing on efforts to limit the loss of life in the near term, which is great. But, as we've discussed, longer-term resolution to most of these issues is directly correlated with educational levels, in particular, literacy levels.

Making sure everyone has the opportunity to learn to read is a hard, long-term investment. Becoming literate is typically a multiyear process. There are no quick fixes. Literacy is a marathon, not a sprint; it's not a flashy cause that quickly demonstrates marketable results.

Because of the difficulties in making literacy learning available at scale, we as a global community need tenacity and commitment, both of which are not common. Philanthropists, governments, and NGOs must adopt a long-term vision and be willing to support an investment in a lot of hard work over a number of years. That vision must include willingness and patience to facilitate trying and refining a number of different approaches. Leadership in literacy requires those who know their cause is large enough to contribute to solutions to a multitude of problems. That's not your average philanthropist, and that's not your average governmental and aid organization.

In the course of my work at Curious Learning, I've had numerous conversations with company foundations and with corporate social responsibility programs. Every now and then I'll be lucky enough to have a one-on-one conversation with someone working in these organizations. Several of them have shared a truth with me—that what they support must align with the business interests of their company. Projects they fund also need to have meaningful results and impacts within a relatively short period of time. I'm grateful to those few who were willing to be so candid. They helped me to better understand the necessary conditions for working with these organizations.

Can we shift this dynamic? Can we cultivate a long-term outlook for how we invest our work and resources? Can we apply that to education? Can societies grow to value helping people become literate, recognizing that literacy is one of the single best ways to help people on multiple levels for the rest of their lives?

Becoming literate is truly empowering. Reading allows you to chart and illuminate your own path, providing access to materials and resources way beyond what you could have imagined before you could read. As an early reader, I can remember excitedly telling my parents about something I had learned from reading a magazine, and the looks of surprise on their faces that I was sharing something with them that they did not know themselves. What a sense of independence and agency. This is particularly true in a world where the Internet and all kinds of devices are increasingly available to most everyone. Reading enables us to develop powers of discernment and critical thinking; it casts light on other worlds and lives, guiding us toward increasing empathy. Reading helps us make informed decisions and creates space to discover truths. The goal of most development and social justice work is to open the way so that others can step into a better life—literacy is one of the most potent tools for doing just that. Literacy nurtures agency, and with agency, we can decide for ourselves what defines a "better" life.

Our mission at Curious Learning is to give everyone the opportunity to learn to read. It is not to get everyone reading. This is a subtle but important nuance. We are working to create opportunities for all, to light the path to literacy. It is incumbent on those we serve to choose to walk this path. We believe literacy is empowering, but we need to first empower people by offering them a choice. We all learn with greater depth and efficiency when we make the choice to engage in learning for ourselves. At Curious Learning, all we want to do is open the way.

———

Back in Ethiopia, at our first lush agrarian community way up in the mountains, the children continued to use the apps and progress on their learning journeys. At the outset of the project, close to twenty children were using the tablets. Four years later, in 2018, we were able to track down six of the original kids and check on their progress. All six of them had acquired a basic level of reading. So the original research question had been answered: Yes, children could absolutely learn to read on their own with nothing more than a set of apps on a mobile device. These children had clearly not only survived but they had also thrived.

The second village, out in the bush, was another story. Over the course of those four years, that area had experienced a major drought. We had returned to learn that the whole village had packed up and left. The village no longer had water. We lost track of them, because they had done what was necessary for their survival. Thriving had become a secondary concern.

———

As a global society, it seems those of us with means often make it a top priority to ensure that people have the opportunity to survive. But, for some reason, we are too often willing to walk away there, instead of facilitating opportunities for true thriving. Why is this? Could it be that those of us who are thriving often find ourselves in positions of power and believe that helping others thrive, too, would jeopardize that power? Or do we believe that everyone must provide for themselves? That others need to be responsible for their own success? That somehow facilitating learning and growth robs others of the opportunity to learn for themselves? We rarely take that attitude when it comes to our own children. Or maybe it is the idea that we are all competing for some limited set of resources. That, in my opinion, truly is a limiting belief. Regardless, I believe the real questions are as follows: How do we shift our belief system so that we all work together to present everyone with the opportunity to thrive, not just survive? And how do we embrace the reality that helping everyone does not hurt anyone? It only helps everyone! As others have said, the right kind of selfishness includes the realization that helping others is the best way to help oneself.

In most rural villages, there is great pressure for children after about the age of ten, if not before, to start to participate in work—taking care of younger siblings, fetching water, tending to the sick, helping with crops. This was indeed the case in both of these Ethiopian villages. If a child has not made significant progress in their literacy journey by age ten, they are very likely never to become literate. For the 600 million children out there in similar situations, the clock started ticking when they reached the age of four. That's when they were developmentally old enough to start learning to read. The next six years of their lives are the crucial window of opportunity if they are to learn to read. The most likely scenario is that they will live their entire lives illiterate, with all the attendant disadvantages of illiteracy.

The stark reality is that we lose an entire generation of children every six years!

In the bush village, we can assume that when drought forced those families to move, the children no longer had access to the tablets and solar charging stations. They were now relegated to lives without reading. The saddest part is that, without them or others in the village being literate, these kids have no way to comprehend just how much of a loss that is. It is incumbent on those of us who have already crossed the bridge of becoming literate and understand the extent of its benefits to do everything we can to help. Every year we wait, we relegate forty million children to lives of illiteracy. And that was before the pandemic.

Reframing Sustainability

Money Is the Fuel for Change,
Not the Goal

Our plane landed in Dhaka, Bangladesh. It was June of 2014, and we had flown overnight, taking an indirect path from Patna, India, via Delhi. We gathered our things, made our way off the plane, then headed toward immigration. The walkway opened out into a larger hall with almost no signage concerning what we should do or where we should go. After wandering aimlessly and asking a few people, we finally found the necessary immigration forms and the end of a single line that snaked through the entire room.

As we waited, I started chatting with the man in line ahead of us. He was a structural engineer who had been making regular trips to Bangladesh. Apparently, some buildings had recently collapsed. He told me that there was a lot of rapid building going on. There were few building codes, and the codes that existed were not enforced. He was there to help inspect buildings, and he told me that, on more than one occasion, he had become so concerned during an inspection that he felt compelled to leave the building immediately and advise others to do so as well. This was already becoming an interesting site visit.

We finally reached the front of the line, where we found a man in a khaki uniform with a semi-groomed beard sitting at a large, old, wooden desk. It was the solid kind of desk your grandfather or great-grandfather would have had in his office, only not so attentively cared for. On the desk was a massive ledger that was nearly the size of the entire desktop.

The man at the desk reviewed our passports and added entries to the massive ledger for each of us. Before stamping our passports, though, he handed them back and asked us in a perfunctory voice, as if this was always part of the process, to check that everything was in order. Everything seemed fine, so we handed them back to him. He briskly flipped through the passports and handed them back to us yet again, again asking that we ensure all was in order. Oh, I thought, he's waiting for some cash to fall out of those passports. Not willing to succumb to bribery, I chose to feign ignorance as we passed the passports back and forth three or four times. At last, exasperated, he explained that we had failed to write the name of the district for the place where we would be staying. There was no place to write this information on the form, and this was clearly information he already knew, didn't actually need, and wasn't going to share with us. He explained that we would need to correct our oversight and return to the back of the line. And so, we headed to the back of the line, figuring we might as well wait there while we looked up the district name and searched for a small space on the form in which to squeeze it.

Eventually, we found ourselves back in front of our old friend, where we continued our charade of naiveté and displayed a sense of pride in our accomplishment of his task. He riffled through the passports once again, this time giving them a good shake. He looked up at us, galled, then, in a grand gesture that required the use of his entire arm, he flipped back through the pages of the massive ledger in search of our names. At long last, he checked us off, and then stamped our passports. It may have taken an extra couple of hours, but we felt gratified to have patiently outlasted him.

Stephanie and I were in Dhaka to meet a new partner, Luke, who had opened the CAFFE (Computers Are Free For Everyone) computing center at the edge of one of the slums there. Luke, formerly a school teacher in England, had visited Dhaka and had become inspired to move there to start a nonprofit to help provide this community with educational opportunities. He had cultivated a trusting relationship with the community, and that trust opened community leaders to the prospect of meeting us and allowing us to test the use of apps for literacy learning. He had also discussed the development of apps in local languages with local and national government officials, and we were excited to hear about that.

We got up the next morning and dressed appropriately for the humidity, heat, and flooded streets—it was the rainy season in this part of the world. Our host took us to CAFFE, the office they had rented on the edge of the slum and transformed into a makeshift learning center where kids could gather and take part in different programs. We observed a series of activities for kids of a range of ages, with a particular interest in the work with younger kids around literacy.

That evening we spent time talking with our hosts, Luke and one of his most active supporters. They explained that there were very few apps for literacy learning in Bengali, the national language of Bangladesh. Luke was teaching kids to read and had a strong interest in developing digital learning tools in Bengali. His group had approached the national government to discuss the kinds of support they might provide, not only for the development of an app but also for its distribution to children nationwide. The government officials were enthusiastic, but there was one significant condition: They wanted images of elected officials' faces to appear prominently and frequently inside the app. I'm sure we looked puzzled when he told us this. We immediately asked why. Apparently, ballots in Bangladesh are printed with both names and photographs of candidates to accommodate high rates of illiteracy among the electorate—only half the population has any literacy skills at all. There was a high correlation between winning an election and the frequency with which the public viewed a candidate's face leading up to the election. Government officials clearly saw the development and dissemination of an app where kids and families were constantly seeing their faces as a perfect vehicle for facilitating their reelection. There was little to no discussion. We all immediately agreed that the government would not be a suitable partner for this work.

The next morning our host took us to meet members of the community and to see where they lived. In typical form for this time of year, the sky opened up and it poured as we weaved in and out of the maze of small streets on foot. By the time we made it to the edge of the community, the rain had let up and the sun was poking out from time to time. We were now wading through a good six to twelve inches of dirty water everywhere we walked. Unable to see through the murky water, we had no idea what, exactly, was beneath our feet. We were glad to be wearing shoes that fully protected our feet and grateful that our tetanus shots were up to date—both things locals didn't necessarily have.

Off the main pathway through the community were eight-foot-wide walkways between homes made of corrugated metal. Each home had an open doorway covered by a curtain made of the local pattern-dyed cloth, mostly in bright colors. At this time of day, curtains were often lashed to the door jambs allowing us a view inside. We turned down a side path to meet some of the community members. A ladder leaned against one of the buildings, and a man wearing a plastic bag on his head to shield him from the rain worked on the roof. He was making some repairs to a leak, more easily found while it was raining. He stopped his work and gazed downward. As our host waved to him, a smile spread across his face.

Exploring the community, I was particularly struck by the bright colors of people's clothing. I could only imagine the amount of work it must have taken to maintain the bright cleanliness of it under these conditions. It was clear that our hosts were well-received by the community. Everywhere we went, they were greeted with smiles, even from the more timid children. What was unique about this urban site compared to the other sites we had visited was the opportunity to work directly with those inside the community in their homes. Some community leaders were excited to support our work and were willing to monitor the use of the devices we planned to hand out. This was the first urban site where we could distribute devices that would stay in the children's homes for them to use and play with at any time. As we finished the day, we left with indelible images and experiences of this community and excitement for how we could work with this partner to provide so much learning for both the children and ourselves.

Reading Is Sustainable and Sustains Us

There is not much in this world as sustainable as having learned how to read. Once you master the task, you do it automatically, rarely reflecting on the process. You use this skill all day every day. It becomes completely incorporated into daily activities. For example, you are doing it right now without even thinking about it.

I sometimes wake up in the morning and set the goal of trying to be aware of every time I use my reading skills—from when I read the messages flowing into my phone, to checking the news highlights, to glancing at the information on the cereal box, to checking the clock. It goes on and on. Try as I may, it is rare that I get more than half-an-hour into my day without having already lost that awareness. My thoughts are rapidly consumed with tasks at hand; I have lost all awareness of the reading

I have been doing in order to check that task off my list. Maintaining that awareness, though, you start to realize that you engage reading skills for almost everything you do. Taking it a step further, you start to understand how different your life would be without reading.

What would that look like?

- With each grade level of literacy, one typically earns 9.7 percent more.[32]
- In the United States, you are 3.5 times more likely to end up in jail if you don't finish high school.[33]
- With basic literacy, one contributes, on average, more than US$1,500 per year to the global GDP for the rest of one's life.[34]

Reading is a fundamental part of everything we do; we can hardly begin to imagine what life would be like without it. In many places, learning to read is basically your full-time job between the ages of four and eight. Yet those four years feel like a drop in the bucket compared to the immense sustained value reading provides over the course of a lifetime.

Can a Nonprofit Be Sustainable by Putting Itself Out of Business?

In July of 2014, we returned to the United States following our visit to Dhaka and the rest of our community visits. By September, we had incorporated Curious Learning and applied for its nonprofit status as a 501(c)(3). Armed with the promise that we could find a way for mobile technology to give everyone the opportunity to learn to read, coupled with the understanding that a literate parent rarely raises an illiterate child, this felt like

---

[32]Dean Jamison and Marco Schäferhoff, "Estimating the Economic Returns of Education from a Health Perspective," Background Paper for the Education Commission. SEEK Development (SEEK), 2016.

[33]Alliance for Excellent Education, *Factsheet: The Impact of Education on Crime* (Author, 2003).

[34]Cree et al., "The Economic and Social Cost of Illiteracy", estimate the global cost of illiteracy to the global GDP at around $1.2 trillion. And the number of illiterate people is approximately 800 million. 1.2 trillion/800 million = $1,500.

a once-in-a-lifetime opportunity to be of service. This actually felt like a once-in-multiple-lifetimes opportunity. What could be more sustainable than bringing a whole generation into literacy and effectively eradicating illiteracy for generations to come?

With Curious Learning founded and a new array of partners and research sites lined up, we started broadening our circle with likeminded individuals and organizations that would be as excited about this opportunity as we were. The size and scale of our project started to catch the eyes of others, especially those in the emerging prosocial investment space. People in this space talked of a double bottom line, centered on strong financial returns and a positive social impact. They wanted to explore Curious Learning becoming a for-profit or a hybrid for-profit entity coupled with a nonprofit. We had a number of these conversations and built out a number of business plans with different revenue strategies, many of them intriguing. But it seemed to always come down to one question: When we find ourselves in a situation where there is a choice between reaching another ten million children or making US$10 million, these investors and partners made it clear they would need to go with the financial return. We decided this would not serve our mission. When we declined, the response was—"How will you be sustainable?"

Over the next year, we were lucky enough to find a group of small family foundations and individuals who were as inspired by our work and its opportunities as we were. We also received a series of research grants. This collection of donors has not only provided a base of financial support, but, in many cases, they have become good friends to both Curious Learning and to me personally.

As a new organization, we continued to reach out to better understand where we fit in the nonprofit ecosystem. Often, a nonprofit is founded to fill a societal gap that for-profit companies or governments are not filling, such as community centers and homeless shelters. It makes sense for nonprofits to fill these gaps—the act of providing certain products or services is not inherently profitable, yet they serve the public good. That is the reason they are given nonprofit status.

The privilege of not paying taxes is a function of working in the service of society and of pledging to not build profit for profit's sake. A nonprofit's revenue is spent in service of its mission. To that end, nonprofits are required to disclose information about their operations and to spend a certain percentage of their revenue or endowment every year to maintain their nonprofit status. There are a few exceptions, like universities and donor-advised funds. One could argue that those exceptions do not serve the interest of society, but that's another topic.

So of these nonprofits, some have a revenue source (like tuition paid to private schools) that covers all or part of their operating expenses. They are still given nonprofit status, because their mission is deemed to be in service to society, and they have pledged to use any excess financial resources for the pursuit of that mission. But Curious Learning is a different type of nonprofit, one that does not have such a revenue stream. We work on behalf of those who do not have the means to pay for the service we provide. We are similar in that way to organizations like The Red Cross and Doctors Without Borders. In Curious Learning's case, that means giving everyone, and, in particular, those below the global poverty line (those making less than US$2 per day), the opportunity to learn to read.

So, what is the traditional path for starting a nonprofit that will rely on philanthropic giving? And, if you start one, how will your organization become sustainable? You have an experience that opens your eyes to a need in your society where you know there is inherently no profit to be made. You articulate the mission and have a plan for realizing it. Now you need to marshal the resources, both staff and financial, needed to make it a reality. So how do you go about raising those funds, and how do you generate a consistent enough cash flow to make your organization sustainable? Most nonprofits end up building a part of their organization to focus on donor acquisition and cultivation. This means your nonprofit ends up spending a not-insignificant percentage of every dollar raised on the task of raising more dollars. Inherently, you have to learn how to build a fundraising operation that allows you to address the issues you started the organization to address.

While this style of fundraising may seem inefficient or like a distraction from an organization's mission, it does work well for certain types of nonprofits. For example, it generally works for locally based nonprofits, where donors within a community make smaller contributions that allow an organization to serve the particular needs of a segment of the community's population. Soup kitchens and community arts centers, among other types of community organizations, may operate this way. In these cases, donors contribute with a focus on the longevity of these nonprofits, hoping to enable them to address community needs that might otherwise never be addressed. Donors view their donations as pure philanthropic gifts, used to sustain work that matters to them. The gift is a way of being of service and giving back to others; more often than not, the donor relishes in their ability to do so and is grateful for their own success, which has allowed them to contribute.

As our exploration brought us into discourse with the larger philanthropic community, a different type of mindset seemed to be emerging. Most of the newer large philanthropic organizations are funded by large amounts of money coming from extremely successful entrepreneurs. In 2010, as many as fifty-seven billionaires signed the giving pledge, promising to contribute most of their wealth to philanthropic causes. Fifteen years later, more than 50 percent of those billionaires were worth even more, indicating that they are making money faster than they are giving it away.[35]

If you look closely at how these large foundations speak about their process, many of them now rely on the word "investment." In some cases, these large philanthropic organizations have set themselves up to be a combination of investor and donor, blurring the line between traditional giving and traditional investing. But, in both cases, they talk about the act of giving money as an "investment," not as a gift. Investment, by definition, is the action of putting a resource, like cash, forward today in the anticipation that it will create some future wealth. So why are they using this term in the context of what traditionally would be philanthropic giving? Here are a few possible explanations that we have explored.

One, they are trying to appropriate the word "investment" to mean an investment in creating a change or a positive impact on the world. This is possible, but I have not seen much evidence of it. And isn't that what philanthropic giving was always about? Why would it need a new word, especially one like "investment," which is already used widely in another context?

---

[35]Institute for Policy Studies, "The Giving Pledge at 15: Unfulfilled, unfulfillable, and not our ticket to a fairer, better future," IPS, 2025, accessed August 21, 2025, https://ips-dc.org/report-giving-pledge-at-15/.

Two, maybe it is code for saying that they want their money (invest-ment) to return some sort of social credibility, a way of saying they are judging whether or not to make a donation based on the successful social track record of an organization, which would reflect positively on them. They, as funders, would be seen as having made a good decision and would receive the appropriate amount of social recognition for having funded a successful and beloved nonprofit. This kind of scenario creates challenges for young nonprofits that have not yet been recognized for their work and have not invested in the public relations needed to es-tablish their social credibility. With a social return as the motivation, a foundation would be loath to donate to these younger nonprofits. They wouldn't take a risk on an organization that could potentially fail and damage their social credibility. Often, by the time a nonprofit reaches the level of success required to attract these large philanthropic foundations, they no longer have the same financial needs they once had.

Interestingly, in most cases, those who start the large foundations have amassed their fortunes by taking great risks in the for-profit sector, and they continue to take great risks in their for-profit investments. They know that real innovation is risky; they are lucky even if only one out of eight for-profit companies they invest in succeeds. But, for some reason, they are incredibly risk-averse when it comes to their philanthropic dona-tions. This impedes innovation in the nonprofit space. It's hard to know if aversion to the potential of damage to a foundation's social credibility drives their aversion to risk when investing in nonprofits; but, if that is the case, no one wants to admit it. It does seem a plausible explanation, though, in light of the behavior we have seen.

A third possibility is that large philanthropic foundations use the word "investment" because it reflects the capitalistic measures that have served them so well in earning massive amounts of money. Perhaps they are most comfortable using the language of capitalism, despite its dis-tance from the tools and methods appropriate for the nonprofit realm. In other words, they're saying, "I don't want to support you indefinitely; you need to be sustainable. I want reassurance that this nonprofit will soon be self-sufficient. I'll only fund you if my investment moves you toward not needing my money." The problem with this approach is that it values the goal of creating a self-sustaining organization over the value of the mission-driven work. The nonprofit feels the pressure to raise more money despite just receiving a grant and will often distort or neglect the mission-driven work to try to land more funding. One of the best gifts a donor can give to an organization is a long-term commitment with the message of, "Now do what you were founded to do."

I think relying on the word "investment" when funding nonprofit organizations misses yet another important point. In for-profit investments, the long-term sustainability of the organization is rarely the focus these days. Instead, the focus is on creating an exit strategy, a time when investors can extract money from the organization, ideally with a significant profit. In the for-profit world, the notion of an exit strategy is desirable. Is there an equivalent for a nonprofit? Some nonprofits begin with the aim of completing a mission (instituting some sort of change). With that done, their work can come to an end. It's an exit of a different kind—one that tends not to be considered a desirable outcome for those making a philanthropic "investment." But what better return is there than completing a mission that benefits society?

The completion of a nonprofit's mission can take different forms. A nonprofit may have developed a new way of doing things that empowers governments to pick up the mission and carry it forward on society's behalf. This would be a nonprofit equivalent of an initial public offering (IPO) or acquisition. Or a mission may be realized and no longer require further investment—the for-profit equivalent of having saturated the market. An example of this would be the polio vaccine and its distribution. Polio vaccines have been distributed throughout the world and the disease has been, for the most part, eradicated. Any nonprofit working to eradicate polio has now, thankfully, become obsolete.

There may be other explanations for the use of the word "investment" among some philanthropists. Regardless, there is a need to rethink what is meant by sustainability and our relationship to it if we are going to support innovation in the nonprofit space and support the success of the missions of nonprofits. The good news is that there seems to be a growing interest in prosocial and nonprofit entrepreneurship that will provide the pressure needed to bring about this shift.

———

Some months after our visit to Dhaka, we were still working out the details of acquiring and deploying devices into the community when we got a message from our partner. He had gotten up one morning, just as he had every morning, and made his way across town to the edge of the community to find all the homes gone or flattened. Everyone he had spent the last years getting to know was gone. Apparently, the landowner had other designs for the land upon which they had set up their homes. His approach, which I later learned was not uncommon, was to hire bulldozers to flatten the communities in the middle of the night, sending the occupants running. This was the best way to clear the land without the inhabitants having the ability to protest or resist. Having no way to contact or find anyone from the community, our host had returned home to England.

As we got off the call, I reflected on our visit and the people we had met. This action certainly showed that the way these people were living was not sustainable. Nonetheless, the few kids who had been able to learn some literacy skills were indeed taking those skills with them. I could not help but think that if we had only managed to get smartphones into the hands of these children, it would have provided a way for them to continue their learning as they were scattered to the wind. How can we work quickly and efficiently enough to avoid losing another generation to illiteracy?

———

Shortly after Curious Learning was founded, we adopted a new resolution that every couple of years we would review whether or not our organization was still needed. In other words, we would ask the following questions: Does every child now have the opportunity to learn to read? As it is rare for a literate parent to raise an illiterate child, has the future generation been given the literacy skills that they will pass on to their children? If the answers were yes, we would shut down: Mission accomplished.

We had decided that the most sustainable thing we could do was to accomplish our mission by helping bring a whole generation into literacy. Then, generation after generation would work to maintain literacy in their families indefinitely. By taking this stance, we were free to create a roadmap and put a price tag and timeline on accomplishing this mission.

We estimated that, at a cost of 25 cents per child and 600 million children, our mission could be accomplished for US$150 million. So, for a one-time cost of US$150 million, we could add as much as US$1.2 trillion to the global GDP year after year. Even if our cost estimates were off by a factor of ten or one hundred or even 1,000, it would still be worth doing. That feels like a good interpretation of sustainability: a mission that has a sustainable impact on the lives of individuals and on the global community, generation after generation, not the creation of another company (nonprofit or not) that works to live forever.

If we had been able to help those children in Dhaka to learn to read, we would at least know that as they were driven from their homes they were leaving with a skill that could never be taken away from them.

By redefining sustainability as being the result of change, we gave ourselves a fighting chance to actually achieve a grand mission. Any grand mission requires change. The good news is that change is inevitable. All things change eventually. But how do you embrace and activate that change and let it propel your mission forward? If we focus on creating organizations that will live forever, we are not embracing inevitable change, and we are not empowering ourselves to affect the change we started the organization to make. I welcome the day when Curious Learning's work is done, and I can reflect and dream about the next change in my life and other's lives that will catalyze our next stage of learning and growth.

Relearning Curiosity

Reframing Failure as Learning

We walked into the classroom to find about a dozen students, mostly graduate students along with a few highly accomplished undergraduates. We introduced ourselves, sharing a little about our backgrounds. The group was diverse—some were studying education, some technology, and others design. I shared that I was excited to be teaching and learning with such a capable group of students, and I acknowledged that their presence in the class was a result of their hard work and success, as demonstrated by, among other things, the number of As on their transcripts. Then I dropped the real message: This class would be different. They would only get an A in the class if at some point (if not multiple points) they were to fail. In other words, the only way to succeed was to fail. They all looked at me with confusion and some with fear. I could see some of them weighing their option to drop the course.

In the early years of Curious Learning, as we were running research studies around the world, we were asked to teach a graduate-level class at Tufts University on the process of designing educational apps for early literacy. My background in technology and user experience design for children and my cofounder and co-teacher's background in the science of how one learns to read, curriculum development, and teacher training had been stirred together for the last few years in a large experimental pot that was spiced by data and observation from around the world. The work we had been doing in the field was shifting and adjusting our thinking about how to best empower learning. How could that not only inform the content of this class but also offer insight into how to structure the learning experience for these graduate students?

The act of designing the user experience and the user interface of any app is deceptively difficult. If your users are preliterate children, the design process is impossible without extensive trial and error. As app designers we rely on a number of techniques to help us do our job. We can usually begin with the assumption that our users have experienced many different apps and, therefore, have learned certain conventions. For example, the user will know that a particular type of graphic is a button, and the word on the button explains what will happen when you touch it. But for pre-literate users, we can make no such assumptions. Young children may not have absorbed the convention of what an on-screen button is, and, even if they have, they can't read the word we place on it.

Going into this class, I had decades of experience designing user interfaces—the graphics, images, and text on the screen—everything experienced from the time a user starts to engage with a product or company to when they finish. I designed mostly for children. Even with all that experience, I had never gotten it right the first time. It always takes many interactions. One reason is that designers need to work to understand the mindset of the user. We pretend we are seeing the user interface for the first time, calling only on knowledge the user would have. The challenge is to closely observe one's own thoughts, hunting for moments when knowledge the user would not have comes into play; at that point, we need to stop ourselves from using that knowledge. Observing oneself in this way is exceptionally difficult, even more so when your user is a young, preliterate child.

Once we know how to read, it becomes so automatic that we read things without being aware of engaging our reading skills. The only practical way to overcome this limitation is to just try things. In other words, design something and devise a way to test it with a sample of the intended audience. Then do your darndest to keep your preconceptions from getting in the way of understanding the data and the observations. In other words, you have to fail and you have to fail a lot.

So, for the students in our class, we needed to shift them into a mindset of experiencing and embracing this sequence of repeated failures. This would go against all the conditioning they had collected from the educational systems they had so successfully navigated to date.

———

Most school systems operate in particular, if not peculiar ways. Take the weekly spelling test that so many of us around the world experienced in our primary school years. You are introduced to a set of words. Then you use and practice those words throughout the week. At the end of the week, you are given a quiz to see how well you can spell them. You get your grade, and the next week comes with its next set of words. If you did well, everything is fine. But, in most cases, if you did poorly (as I often did), there is no reflection on how to improve, no time to revisit or even master those words. You just fail. Certainly for me (and I think my teachers as well), after a few weeks of this, I came to the conclusion that I was a bad speller. I still feel that way forty-five years later. The only difference is I now have a computer correcting me as I type.

Most school systems cycle between times of instruction and times of evaluation (or testing). The evaluations find those students who successfully absorb and repeat (or at times apply) the information they were given. Then students are advanced and given more instruction. Those who mastered the previous material demonstrate that they are receiving the instruction they are ready for. For the most part, those who have not fully mastered the material are pulled along as well. More often than not, their ability to master any material becomes progressively challenged as new material builds on the previous material they have not yet mastered. In low-income countries, the majority of students either drop out of school or reach an exit level (often at the seventh grade or, if they are lucky, the twelfth grade). In sub-Saharan Africa, 42 percent of children drop out of school by the end of primary education. Even when they do reach an exit grade, they rarely have all the skills one would hope they would have acquired by reaching that level of education. Even in the United States, where there are systems in place to help struggling readers, the average American reads at a seventh-grade level, and 30 million adults read at or below a fifth-grade level.

In this structure, intermittent tests become a way for societies to know how many students are succeeding, but they are rarely used to inform or improve the educational process. Tests separate the "successful" students from the "unsuccessful" students, hence the term "high-stakes" tests, or tests used to determine whether or not a student progresses. By default, this system sorts out successful students, and their numbers dwindle as they move through the education system, from primary to secondary to university to advanced degrees. Once you get past a secondary education, those high-stakes tests become gatekeepers to accessing further education. Embedded in this system is the belief that the educational process is about finding those who have certain innate or cultivated abilities and empowering them to play a role in society. The result is a kind of winnowing.

In the context of a society that has limited resources and wants to apply those resources to those students with the most potential, you can see how this structure has been an asset. But global society is changing and with it the relationship of the individual to education. So does this approach still meet our needs? Will it help us achieve the new goals we are setting?

In 2015, the member-countries of the UN adopted seventeen SDGs. These goals were set in an effort to "end all forms of poverty." Goal Number 4 (SDG4) ensures inclusive and equitable quality education and promotes lifelong learning opportunities for all.

SDG4 is a very public statement that education is now perceived as a human right and a fundamental way to assist and support anyone and everyone's ability to move out of poverty. The most important thing to note here is that global society now believes that not only can everyone learn but that everyone has the right to learn. This is fundamentally different from the practice of filtering students based on performance. Yet our current approach to education often selects from among and promotes particular students instead of ensuring and promoting learning opportunities for all. Students often end up experiencing failure as a stopping point instead of as an informative part of the learning process that would allow them to continue their learning journey.

Many foundations, including some of the largest in the world, focus a huge amount of resources on creating scholarship opportunities. The recipients are people who would otherwise never have access to better private schools or higher levels of education. These scholarships are a real gift to these people. When scholarships are given to people from underserved geographic areas, low socioeconomic status, or people with backgrounds that have left them excluded, they play an important role in helping to create a more just and balanced society. It is important to note, though, that these programs work within the confines and structures of the current educational system. It is also worth noting that foundations use their own selection processes; they find and select those they support, and often that is coupled with the need for the student to attain admission to a school. These opportunities are inherently not for everyone.

So here we have it: The member-states of the UN have proclaimed the new belief that everyone, globally, has the right to quality education, yet the systems we have in place to achieve this only serve a subset of the population. Over the last decade, there have been heroic efforts to enroll as many children in school as possible. This has been particularly success-ful in India's Education for All program. Since 2001, the program has brought nearly 20 million children into primary school; it now caters to some 200 million children across the country.[36]

Giving access to everyone is a great first step, but the approach and structure of systems of education have not changed. Enrolling everyone in school gets everyone to the starting line, but it does not ensure that everyone will run a full race. In 2015, South Africa's educational system had reason to celebrate: Approximately 76 percent of high school students had managed to pass final exams. But a researcher quickly pointed out that twelve years earlier, in 2003, around 1 million students had started school and just over half of them (550,127) had made it to the exams.[37] So, in reality, only about 55 percent had passed. How do we not continue to fall into this trap?

Can we effectively catalyze learning for everyone? Research is begin-ning to yield a clearer understanding of how. Our work at Curious Learn-ing, curating apps and online activities that promote literacy learning, has been greatly informed by neuroscience and behavioral research over the last few decades. Many researchers, including Stephanie, have spent years studying those who struggle to learn to read, like those with dyslexia, as compared with others. This comparison provides insights into how peo-ple learn to read and helps define what educators can do to support those

---

[36]World Bank Group, "Educating India's Children," September 18, 2015, https://www.worldbank.org/en/country/india/brief/educating-india-children

[37]Department of Basic Education, "Education Sector Review: 2015–2016," Republic of South Africa, 2016, accessed February 19, 2025, https://www.agsareports.co.za/wp-content/uploads/2022/09/Education-Sector-Report-2015-16.pdf; also see K. Wilkinson, "The Flaw in SA's 'Real' Matric Pass Rate Figure (as Calcu-lated by the EFF and DA)," *Africa Check*, January 9, 2018, https://africacheck.org/fact-checks/spotchecks/flaw-sas-real-matric-pass-rate-figure-calculated-eff-da.

struggling to learn. This research has also identified subskills that need to be developed and practiced. Our current understanding is that direct and scaffolded, or supported, incremental instruction allows children to practice these newly understood subskills to help everyone learn to read. It is true that some may need more time and exposure to fully master those skills, but what works for dyslexic children works for all children learning to read. There are ways to create instructional methods that help everyone. This suggests that, as we better understand the underlying mechanisms of learning to read, we will be better equipped to build educational systems that will help everyone acquire this necessary skill.

Curiosity and Learning

A decade ago, a neuroscience paper[38] reported on research on the workings of curiosity. A number of adult test subjects were shown a series of questions and were asked to rank their level of curiosity about the answer to each question. As they were being asked, their brains were being scanned. Researchers were able to correlate expressions of curiosity with brain activation patterns. Ten days later, the subjects were asked to return to the lab and answer the same sets of questions. The results showed consistent patterns of activation for levels of curiosity and better memory of items that inspired greater curiosity. The subjects who exhibited higher overall levels of curiosity were also better able to remember the answers for items about which they'd had little curiosity.

It's no surprise that there was a very high correlation between people being curious and remembering the answers to the questions. We all have had the experience of learning things more quickly and with more excitement because we were curious about the material. What was striking was they also saw the same high correlation with the answers to questions they were not curious about. If the person was in a curious state of mind, they were more capable of absorbing the information that was presented to them, even if that information had not inspired curiosity. This paper

---

[38]M. J. Gruber, B. D. Gelman, and C. Ranganath, "States of Curiosity Modulate Hippocampus-Dependent Learning via the Dopaminergic Circuit," *Neuron* 84, no. 2 (2014): 486–96. https://doi.org/10.1016/j.neuron.2014.08.060.

suggests that once we enter a curious state of mind, brain chemistry is activated to facilitate absorbing or remembering information. The brain is ready to reinforce the neural pathways needed to retain that information. Therefore, being curious alone facilitates learning, even when you are curious about something other than what you are learning.

While we have not done research directly into this phenomenon, it does resonate with what we have seen in our field studies with children. In the early years of Curious Learning, we had hundreds of children across a dozen locations in half-a-dozen countries, all of them in impoverished communities, using apps on tablets. Most of the time, we gave these tablets to children with little to no instruction about how to use them. It was their own curiosity that activated their interest to explore, figure out how to turn the tablets on, and navigate to different apps. A curated set of apps that was chosen to help develop early literacy skills was on each tablet. The tablets were set up to constrain, or sandbox, the children to a specific set of educational materials. In all cases, the students' learning curves were steeper than we expected, and they learned as fast, if not faster than an average child in a well-resourced U.S. school generally would have over the same period of time. Their curiosity was driving their learning.

Even though our studies have not been designed to analyze curiosity's impact on learning, a collaborating researcher completed an unpublished analysis on some of our early data.[39] He used interaction data to look at ways in which children explored the apps on the tablets. Children who explored different apps and explored those apps in different sequences had large improvements in a pre-/post-assessment of early literacy skills. If this kind of exploration is a proxy for measuring the mindset of curiosity, then this preliminary data suggest that a more curious, explorative mindset facilitates faster learning. And it seems that children come to it naturally. Many children, when first given the tablets, looked to the teachers to guide them. Once they realized they had to figure it out for themselves, they did just that. And as they made "mistakes," they did not feel judged; they just kept trying different things. Interpreting failure as a bad thing

---

[39]In an unpublished analysis of tablet use by a group of U.S. preschoolers, identification of rhyme and uppercase letters was highly correlated with exploratory behavior between apps (G. Gordon, personal communication, December 9, 2020).

in the learning process, rather than as simple corrective feedback, seems to be a learned behavior. If this is true, we might choose not to teach children to avoid curiosity and potential failure and, instead, create space for them to engage curiosity without repercussions.

We chose the name Curious Learning for our nonprofit before we had seen the neuroscience research on curiosity. We felt it spoke to our own desire to activate the natural curiosity of children that motivates them to learn. But it also spoke about us and our own curiosity about what kinds of new learning paradigms could help achieve the goal of giving everyone the opportunity to learn to read, a goal that we feel is a necessary and important starting point for achieving the UN's goal concerning education for all. The farther we travel on this learning journey, the more apt the name seems to be.

At Curious Learning, we are part of a larger community that is trying to do something that has never been done before: We are promoting lifelong learning opportunities for all. When trying to do something that has never been done before, you have to be free to experiment. You take your best guess and try something, and you collect observations and data to better understand how it does and doesn't work. We entered this journey not knowing what would work, and, for the most part, we are still on that journey of experimentation. The only way we are going to be successful is to remain open-minded and curious, to be curious learners.

––––––

Four weeks into our class on app design for early literacy, our students had gone through the concept design process. Each small group had its concept and codified it on paper. The next step would have been for them to mock up these designs for user testing. When I reviewed what these groups had done, I knew each of them was capable of doing better work. More importantly, what was holding them back was their own attachment to what they had created. If they did not let go of this attachment, they would never fully embrace the curious and experimental mindset that was so necessary to succeed in this project. If they could not embrace this mindset, they would struggle to see what was working and what was not working, even when the data and observations were in front of them. The dilemma was how to help them shift their perspective.

This first month of the class had been a rapid set of activities to guide the concept design process. These activities included defining their goals, articulating those clearly, and then iteratively working to manifest them in a design concept. This had been a lot of new material and a foreign process for most. They entered the classroom nervous and excited to hear how their hard work had been received. They had produced a lot of good work, and we reviewed it project by project. But then I threw a wrench in their thinking and into the syllabus. I explained to them that I now wanted them to discard everything they had just done. I wanted them to start over with a blank slate and take the next week to develop an entirely new design. Their faces dropped in dismay and confusion. I later learned that some of them wondered if it was too late to drop the class. After the out-cries of "How do you expect us to do in one week what took us a month to do before?", they settled and left the classroom a little less shell-shocked.

A week later, I sat in the classroom as the students arrived for the next class. There was a palpable difference in energy. They came in ex-cited and chattering among themselves. Most of them had new ideas and dammed-up energy they were excited to release by sharing these new de-signs. After making space for each group to share their new work, I noted that these new designs were so much clearer and full of new vitality. I asked how the last week and this process had been for them. Their an-swers were imbued with that same excitement: "I had no idea how much we had learned until we had to apply it again over the last week." And, "This new design is so much better; I am so much more excited about it."

It had been freeing for them to let go of their old ideas, allowing themselves to experiment with new ones and to expand their horizons of what was possible. They had moved from, "I just submitted an assign-ment, and I am waiting to hear the teachers' reactions to it" to "I have created something I'm really excited about, and I can't wait to try it out." They were no longer doing the work as just another assignment for a class; they were now excited to experiment and find the best way to bring their ideas into reality.

This continued to serve them well for the rest of the class. As they tested their prototypes, they now opened themselves more easily to what was working and what was not. They showed a new willingness to repeat-edly engage the thought exercise of letting go of what had been created and ask if there was a better way, sometimes coming to a change and sometimes reinforcing the value of what they had done. The more a student had embraced the throw-out-and-redesign process in the fifth week of the class, the more in flow they were with the rest of the class and the more open they were to the process of testing and adjusting their apps. They had adopted an experimental attitude that embraced failure, or at least what is traditionally called failure. They had redefined failure as learning. So much so that they had created a class motto: "Fail fast and fail often!" Every rough patch they could find was a place to be polished, and, now, they were actively seeking out rough patches.

———

Games in general and apps in this case are designed to engage the experimental mindset. That is what makes them so much fun and exciting to play. Designers talk about creating an experience that puts the user in a state of "flow," where the user knows about 75 to 80 percent of what to do, and they need to play or experiment to figure out the balance. When people are in this state of flow, they are most engaged, enjoying the game, and learning the most.[40] The classic structure of a game gives you a level to master. You play that level and fail repeatedly. You are not pushed on to the next level (or even allowed to go to the next level) until you master this one. You try different things, you experiment until you succeed, and then you move on. This is what makes it fun—learning by experimentation. There is an interesting parallel between being an educational apps designer and being a learning user of that app. To make an app that successfully engages the user's learning by experimentation, you as the designer need to work from that experimental mindset.

This experimental mindset can clearly be seen in the children at our research sites. On one of our visits to one of our longest running research

---

[40] This is very similar to a concept that a psychologist by the name of Lev Vygotsky introduced. He defined the notion of a zone of proximal development (ZPD). There is a zone of skills just beyond those that the student has mastered that are the next best ones for them to learn. By providing students support in this zone, you can help them maximize their learning. L. S. Vygotsky, *Mind in Society: The Development of Higher Psychological Processes* (Harvard University Press, 1978).

sites in KwaZulu-Natal, South Africa, I sat outside the early learning center. Kids were scattered around, each with a mobile device and using an app that we had recently localized to isiZulu. This app taught the letters and the sounds they make. As I watched over the shoulder of one of the girls, she clearly knew enough to cruise through the first levels. She would often look back to proudly show me (or at least make sure I was watching) what she had achieved. Then she came to a level where she didn't know what to do. She repeatedly played the level over and over. She became completely absorbed, without any regard to my presence. Eventually, she figured it out and shook her fist in the air in her moment of triumph. We have seen this same pattern repeated in different countries and with different apps around the world. The children easily tap into their innate curiosity and just experiment. They never even consider that not knowing the answer is a failure.

The only way we are going to meet the audacious goals of ensuring and promoting learning for all is by experimenting with our learning systems and processes. We must open ourselves to new ways of reaching everyone and activating learning in them. We must take the leap of trying something new, examine the results, learn from our failures, and activate our successes. We must let go of all ego and preconceptions. We want our students to take risks and not end their learning journey when they fail. We want that perceived failure to reactivate the learning journey. We should be brave enough to do the same.

All of life is learning and growth, and the most joyful way to engage is with a curiosity that reframes failure as part of the learning process. Can our educational systems evolve to take this same approach?

Reach and Learn

The Power of Reframing Even One Belief

It had not been long since we'd turned off the highway, but we quickly found ourselves on a dirt road. We still had at least a half-hour before we would reach the small town of Geluksburg at the base of the Drakensberg Mountains in KwaZulu-Natal, South Africa. It was slow-going as we periodically felt the rumble of our tires over washboard roads, but not as slow as it would have been had it been raining. Rain transforms the clay on the road into a slippery mud, which produces tricky driving conditions where cars tend to slide off roads.

We finally found ourselves back on smooth pavement, only to be forced to stop: Cattle had decided it was time to graze on the other side of the road. After the cattle had made their way across the road, we traveled another 200 meters before turning off the pavement again to head toward our destination. Even if we had continued, the pavement would have lasted only another 100 meters. The crossroads in town are the only paved roads, and they are each only paved for a few hundred meters.

It was a gorgeous, rural setting. Not many people traveled here, only the occasional hiker or mountain biker. There was one small inn and a coffee shop, and both were extensions of the owner's home. For the most part, the community members lived on the surrounding Zulu tribal land.

Our host,[41] Creesen Naicker, was a cofounder of a sports-for-development program that was running throughout a number of communities in South Africa, including this one. The program had been very successful in developing leadership skills, social-emotional skills, and self-confidence among children. But he had realized that, as these kids

---

[41]Little did we know at the time, but years later Creesen would play a role in finding the cracks described in Chapter 2. He became our director of partnerships, the one who excitedly identified being "between a rock and a hard place."

went out into the world with these new skills, they still could not get a job, mainly because they could not read adequately. So he started searching for a way to add literacy learning to the programs. Much to our good luck, he found us.

We had come here to better understand how our work might support the work of our local partners. They ran programs to support the educational and personal development of children and young people in the community. South Africa, much like most of sub-Saharan Africa, has an early education problem. Only 22 percent of children read at grade level by the time they get to fourth grade. Our job was to explore how the work in literacy learning with mobile devices could supplement the educational programs they were starting to build. The hope was that we could not only improve the literacy rate in the community but that we could develop a long-term relationship where we could follow the program's longitudinal impact over many years. Could we, with our partners' help, reach these kids with literacy learning apps, and would reaching them turn into learning over time?

———

Curious Learning's mission was (and still is) to give everyone the opportunity to learn to read. Everyone included children like these, who lived in more rural and impoverished communities. But how could we put this mission into action? What goals would we work toward to achieve this mission? We had two important questions: Could we reach children in need? And would our methods help them learn to read? Regardless of what methodologies or interventions are tried—be they books, schools, smartphone apps, chewing gum and wire, duct tape—nothing will serve any mission unless you can get the thing you're using (tablets, in this case) into the hands of those you wish to reach (children, in this case). For our mission, those children also have to be inspired to use the tablets and hopefully learn something along the way.

This is not to say that other activities are not of value. We, as a society, have for decades, if not centuries, engaged in building up systems to support our desire for education to be available to everyone. Schools, curricula, teachers, ministries of education, all are the result of genuine efforts to create interventions that enable children to learn. If we want to open ourselves to the possibility of new approaches to childhood education, we need to articulate our goals as simply and clearly as possible, and without preconception. And, with that, we need to examine the beliefs we hold and evaluate their worthiness in supporting our goals. In my experience, concise, simple statements are most effective for stating goals. Counterintuitively, the more concise and simple the statement, the more challenging it can be to articulate.

For Curious Learning, the simplest way to state our goals is:

1. To reach children
2. For those children to learn

The value of any other activity or aspiration can be evaluated in relationship with these two primary goals. Everything may be considered— even the roles of schools and teachers are up for debate or may be redefined, which may sound like heresy. By distilling our goals to their essence, we notice assumptions we have made, assumptions that may have solidified into beliefs. We are free to step outside the boxes we have unwittingly inhabited; we can remove the blinders that narrow our vision, opening us to opportunities and alternatives. We can free ourselves to seek new ideas, just as we examine old approaches and beliefs, and we can evaluate them using a new, simplified rubric. We can simply ask: Do the methods we are using help us reach children? Do they help them learn in the most efficient way? Undoubtedly, this process may demonstrate that certain long-held beliefs are either no longer helpful or are in need of some modification. By regularly taking ourselves through this process, we stay open to new opportunities and discover renewed excitement and focus for the work.

Armed with new insights that emerge from simplifying our goals, we review beliefs we have adopted at Curious Learning, as well as other beliefs that originated in previous chapters of our lives, and we examine them through this lens. For every belief, we ask, "Does this method or way of thinking help us reach children?" If yes, "Does it help them learn?"

Even before Curious Learning was founded, the early research project leading up to it was interested in how and if mobile technology could be used to help children learn to read. So you could say that Curious Learning was founded on the belief that:

> *Mobile technology can be used to give everyone the opportunity to learn to read.*

It would be more correct to say that Curious Learning was founded on the question of whether this belief was worth pursuing. Initially, we felt we did not have enough information to judge the value of this belief, and so our first step was to acquire that information. Therefore, much of our work to date has been a process of evaluating the value and validity of this belief through research and experimentation.

Learning: Can Mobile Technology Help?

To jump to the punchline, we believe that mobile technology can help with learning.[42] The first early research site in rural Ethiopia showed that children using tablets with sets of curated apps could learn with no other educational intervention. After one year, the children in the villages were able to read at the same level they would have if they had been in a well-resourced U.S. kindergarten. Field studies over the following year showed that the same steep learning curve could be seen under a variety of circumstances across six countries and over a dozen research sites.[43] These

---

[42]There is a growing base of studies that show how mobile technology can be an effective learning media when used appropriately. Here are just a few: N. L. Saine, M.-K. Lerkkanen, T. Ahonen, A. Tolvanen, and H. Lyytinen, "Computer-Assisted Remedial Reading Intervention for School Beginners at Risk for Reading Disability," *Child Development* 82 (2011): 1013–28. https://doi.org/10.1111/j.1467-8624.2011.01580.x; R. D. Silverman, K. Keane, E. Darling-Hammond, and S. Khanna, "The Effects of Educational Technology Interventions on Literacy in Elementary School: A Meta-Analysis," *Review of Educational Research* (2024, July): 1–41. https://doi.org/10.3102/00346543241261073; L. V. Sánchez-Vincitore and A. H. Cross, "Effects of an Electronic Game on Early Literacy Skills," *Psicologia Escolar e Educacional* 25 (2021). https://doi.org/10.1590/2175-35392021225567.

[43]C. Breazeal, R. Morris, S. Gottwald, T. Galyean, and M. Wolf, "Mobile Devices for Early Literacy Intervention and Research with Global Reach," *Proceedings of the Third (2016) ACM Conference on Learning @ Scale—L@S '16*, 2016, https://doi.org/10.1145/2876034.2876046.

early studies provided lots of usage data that helped us understand which apps children engaged with and subsequently learned from.

This raises an important point: Children need to be engaged in the content before they can learn. The data clearly showed that not all apps are created equal. Some are much more engaging than others. When children are absorbed in the gameplay of the apps, they will spend a lot of time with the material. These insights allowed us to hone in on the right apps to invest in for the sake of further studies and for localization to different languages.

There have been several subsequent studies of the use of these newly developed apps. One study with Syrian refugees, supported by UNICEF and the World Bank, showed that twenty-two hours of access to the Feed the Monster app equated to approximately two months of literacy learning in a well-resourced U.S. school. The World Bank ran a large, randomized control trial in northern Nigeria that shows that children who use apps increase basic literacy skills by 50 percent over the control group.[44]

Given the right apps, mobile technology can indeed help children learn to read. Effective apps also prove to accelerate learning in general. Not only can apps be used on their own, when traditional school is not available, but they can also be used in conjunction with schooling, amplifying and accelerating learning.

Reaching Children: Can Mobile Technology Help?

Can mobile technology, in particular smartphones, be used to reach children, including those most in need? How available is this technology in the areas of the world with the highest levels of illiteracy? To review some figures: 75 percent of all illiterate adults live in India and sub-Saharan Africa. In these areas as of 2025, close to 60 percent of adults already have a smartphone, and it is projected to reach market saturation by 2050 if

[44]Victor Hugo Orozco Olvera and Ericka G. Rascon Ramirez, *Improving Enrollment and Learning Through Videos and Mobiles: Experimental Evidence from Northern Nigeria (English)* Policy Research working paper No. WPS 10413; Impact Evaluation series. (World Bank Group, 2023). http://documents.worldbank.org/curated/en/099446204182379796/IDU0b5f8c3270fed204eeb0a99b0973dd775f03d.

not sooner.[45] The marketplace is making sure that the adoption of this new technology is accelerating at a phenomenal rate and driving down the cost of smartphones. In 2020, smartphones were available for as little as US$30. So the technological infrastructure is being paved. How do we use it to enable literacy learning?

There are a number of organizations providing devices, some to be used in the classroom and some subsidized devices to be handed out to individuals. While there are a number of logistical issues to overcome with this approach, it is still economical, and will be even more so as the cost of devices drops. But the real test of getting to scale and getting there quickly would be tapping those devices parents already have or are soon to buy or receive.

Toward this end, we have been working with partners on a number of distribution strategies—and by distribution we mean encouraging parents to install literacy learning apps on their smartphones and to make those apps available to their children. By the end of the first quarter of 2021, we had run a few dozen tests, which could be broadly organized into two types: the direct-to-parent approach and the approach via a trusted source.

The direct-to-parent approach involved engaging in advertising—something that is rarely applied to educational interventions but is used widely in other arenas. We designed and created a series of ads directed at adults that promoted the awareness of and value of the use of literacy apps among children. In the same way that we had localized the first app to fifty-plus languages, we adapted these ads to local languages as well. This allowed us to target certain regions and demographics using their mother tongue. By advertising on Google and Facebook, we managed to reach large numbers of learners at low cost. Measuring in cost-per-download,

---

[45]It is difficult to find smartphone penetration numbers, but the average of several sources put the levels in 2023 at 51% for SSA and 72% in India. Suggesting that the combined average at around 58% and growing rapidly. https://www.statista .com/statistics/1229799/india-smartphone-penetration-rate/#:~:text=In%20 2023%2C%20the%20penetration%20rate,India%20was%20around%20 144.3%20 million; GSMA, "The Mobile Economy: Sub-Saharan Africa 2023," 2023.https://www.gsma.com/solutions-and-impact/connectivity-for-good /mobile-economy/wp-content/uploads/2024/05/ME-SSA-2023.pdf.

costs varied from 2 cents to 20 cents per download. Approximately 80 to 90 percent of those who downloaded and installed the app opened it and started using it. As an example, in 2021, in Bangladesh, we spent US$111.99 over ten days on targeted advertising on Facebook. The result was 5,398 installs.

It is clear that advertising and social media provide great opportunities to not only reach parents and children but also to promote continued learning and to influence social norms around education. We are starting to build experiments to promote the continued use of our first app, Feed the Monster, and, even more, to promote new apps as mastery is reached or engagement falls off. In this way, we are not only reaching learners, but we are also maintaining engagement, which encourages continued learning. The World Bank is studying the use of social media campaigns to influence and adjust social norms around education, especially where girls' access to education is concerned. We look forward to collaborating with them on further work in this area.

The second approach we tested for reaching children was via trusted sources. We considered trusted sources to be organizations that had relationships with and were trusted by parents. Examples were schools, teachers, ministries of education, employers, and NGOs. NGO partners may not have been working in education, but they were trusted for the other services they provided, like food and healthcare.

Here is how it worked. These trusted sources espoused the value of these apps and provided information or opportunities to install them. This could be done in person at community gatherings or in messages sent by text or WhatsApp to groups of community members. Preliminary results suggested that the upfront cost of this approach over advertising could be higher—the cost-per-download around 50 cents to US$3.90, taking into account staff time and training to run the campaign. However, a much higher percentage of people downloaded the apps and were more likely to spend extended time with them without needing follow-up communications. Staff time and training costs could be amortized over a larger number of downloads if this approach were scaled up.

The two primary methods of outreach we tested, social media ads and text messages, are only available when using mobile technology. So, the mobile technology we use to deliver educational content is the same technology we use to reach our target audience—parents and children. We are only at the beginning of this journey, and there is much more experimentation to be done. At least for now, we have checked both boxes: Mobile technology helps us reach children, and it helps those children learn.

Using mobile technology provides another large advantage, and that is the stream of data back to us. Even when these data are completely anonymous, as it is in our case, they provide great insights. We can monitor how effective we are at reaching our audience and how well they are learning over time. Starting at the beginning of a campaign, we can track how many people see an ad or receive a text message and what percentage of them act on it to download an app. Over time, these data allow us to follow any cohort group and see how engaged they are and how much learning is happening. We are also able to set up A and B groups, testing two different ads, campaigns, or apps, for example, head to head to compare their effectiveness in both reaching kids and helping them learn. This is extremely powerful, and it is not the norm in education.

Traditionally, education researchers might study a particular approach or intervention over years. Then, based on its success, that approach would be released and rarely studied again. This is understandable considering the cost and effort of traditional approaches, which often include printing books, training teachers, and shipping materials, among other things. But technology-driven approaches have a superpower that is transforming so many things in our lives. Companies like Amazon, Uber, and Facebook A/B test different interfaces, campaigns, and pricing on us every day in an effort to optimize their goal of maximizing revenue. Why shouldn't we activate these new tools to help with our goals of reaching children and helping them learn?

Because the data are continuously flowing back, we can interpret and interact with the data quickly. We can use this system to keep adjusting the approach and even adjust for different populations. It becomes a positive feedback loop. For example, we can take a new app that teaches a particular skill and run a campaign to get it into the hands of the children who need it or who are ready for it. The data indicate whether or not the campaign and the app were effective. These data guide our evaluation of the apps and the alterations we might make to them. Do the kids use the app? If so, what parts of it? Do they learn from it? If so, which of their skills improve? Can or should this app be changed to improve its effectiveness, or should it be abandoned? What have we learned from the data that can inform the development of new apps?

This process holds us accountable to our basic goals—to reach children and help them learn.

It also opens the doors for anyone and everyone to contribute and try something new. No one group, be it defined by profession, geography, race, economics, or social status, holds the key to the educational process. Innovation flows out of the many, not the few. Most importantly, this process promotes an experimental mindset. It provides iterative improvement, allowing us to learn, to experiment, and to improve the system over time. As we encourage learning among children, this process asks, and demands, even, that we be curious learners too.

———

Back to the dirt roads and pastoral beauty of our small town at the base of the Drakensberg Mountains in KwaZulu-Natal, South Africa: This was a place where we could practice our approach, even before we had the scale of distribution and the data infrastructure needed for the scale. We returned pretty much every year, brought new apps or new versions of apps, sat on the floors of classrooms for hours as the children used them, and took the long walk home with some of the children through the fields and between the Nguni cows with the occasional hop over a stream to meet and talk with their parents under their thatched roofs. Localizing the apps to isiZulu, the local language, became a priority. This proved to be a way for us to test our localization process, just as it was a way to provide the children with exposure to text in their mother tongue. In the English-speaking world, we are accustomed to vast quantities of children's books always at our disposal. Children may be surrounded by opportunities to explore the written word at a variety of reading levels. That is not the case in isiZulu.

After our first visit to this small town, we returned to Durban, the largest city in KwaZulu-Natal, and decided to use some of our surplus travel budget to buy some isiZulu children's books for the classrooms. At one of the larger bookstores, we found shelves and shelves of children's books, but only a small section devoted to children's books in isiZulu. We bought one copy of every children's book in isiZulu, maybe thirty titles, a small enough number that we could carry them all under one arm. We asked the store manager about other children's books in isiZulu. After searching on her computer, she confirmed that, as far as she could tell, these were all the titles in print and available to order. Can you imagine being able to hold all the children's books available in your language in one hand? This is the case for most of the languages with the largest illiterate populations.

In addition to the warm greetings that included the local three-step handshake and shoulder bump (regular handshake, then shift to holding around each other's thumbs, back to the regular handshake, and while holding hands lean in and bump your right shoulders), we learned so much from these visits. We learned how to optimize and improve the process of localizing apps to new languages, what parts and aspects of the apps most engaged the children, what relationship the children and parents had to the learning-to-read process, and how many people had smartphones and how they might promote the use of the apps within the community.

During one trip, we brought a half-dozen smartphones that we had loaded with a new app. After using them with the children, we decided to give them to members of the community. The understanding was that it would be their job to talk to parents who had smartphones and show them the app. When possible, they could use a program like SHAREit to load the app onto the parent's phone for their children to use. At the time, we had no way to track the impact or number of installs, but we did see a steady increase in the downloads of the isiZulu version of the app over the months to come. We can only speculate that the awareness that grew organically as a result of the effort of these few people greatly contributed to that increase.

A few years after our first visit, I stood outside the learning center in KwaZulu-Natal on a beautiful sunny day, taking a break as the children ran around on the playground. A young woman hobbled into the entrance assisted by a family member. She had been severely injured. The family member found a spot off to the side for her to sit, and, after a conversation with one of the staff members, she returned to the young woman to comfort her. As the hubbub settled, I learned that the staff had called for a vehicle to take her to the closest medical center. They did what they could to support her as she waited. I realized quickly that the work being done here had become extremely effective at reaching the members of the community—so much so that the learning center had become a trust center for the community, where people could get the help and support they needed. This showed a whole different level of reach, above and beyond what was supported by the great attendance numbers the center had. They certainly had achieved the goal of reach. Now, the question was, were the children learning?

Approximately four years after our first visit, a small longitudinal study was done to look at the learning impact these programs had on literacy. In November of 2019, fourth graders from the program were tested. The results were astounding. All of these children, 100 percent of them, were able to read for meaning in isiZulu. This was compared to the national average of 22 percent. In South Africa, schools switch from the local language to English as the language of instruction at the fourth grade, so the children were also tested in English. In English, their second language, they scored twice the national average for fourth graders. Clearly, our partners had done a remarkable job. They had built a youth sports program that fully engaged the community and expanded it in a number of ways to provide effective literacy learning. It is impossible to know the extent of the impact the apps we provided had on these outcomes, as they were only one piece of many in the puzzle that created this incredible picture. But, in the long run, does it really matter? These children were reached and they learned!

These outcomes establish the groundwork for a new generation of fully literate community members with the ability to pass literacy on to future generations.

Limiting Beliefs

Reframe to Transform Limiting Beliefs

Our host, Ester Makumbi, was kind enough to pick us up. The night before, after arriving at Entebbe International Airport, we had stayed at a local hotel near her home, just southwest of Kampala, Uganda. This June morning in 2014 was sunny, and people were buzzing around, trying to get things done during the cooler part of the day. Ester drove us to her house, where she had set up the Clover School.

From her minivan window, I observed the activities along the street, which was filled with traffic and drivers vigorously honking their horns. This main road was only two lanes wide and, while paved, was often covered with the red dirt or mud tracked onto it from unpaved intersecting roads. After passing a few larger intersections with vendors selling their wares, including local deep-fried grasshoppers that are surprisingly like potato chips in texture and saltiness, we turned onto a dirt road. Soon, we came to a deeply rutted section of road I would have questioned navigating even in a 4x4; our intrepid host proceeded nonchalantly in her old minivan, seemingly unconcerned by how close we came to getting stuck on multiple occasions. As we reached her house, she honked the horn and someone opened the gate. The children knew to move out of the way. She pulled in and parked beside the front yard that was set up as a playground with unique and creative pieces of play equipment made from found objects.

Only months earlier, we had met some of Ester's supporters at a cafe in Cambridge, Massachusetts. We learned from them that, in Uganda, the school system is separated into public schools and inexpensive private schools. It sounded like the public school provided little to no educational value. If a child wanted a shot at an education, they would need to pass an admissions test for the private school system. This entailed testing their ability to read in English at the age of six. So, at a typically preliterate age, children needed to have some basic reading skills in a language they typically did not speak. The absurdity of this was not lost on Ester. She had children of her own for which she had needed to navigate this system. As she watched the disparity in opportunities available to children like her own versus children of families living in nearby slums, she felt compelled to offer help. She felt that she could have the biggest impact by giving these children the opportunity to prepare for the private school admissions exam. She turned her home into a preschool where children ages three to six could come, receive a meal or two, and start their journey to literacy.

For a few months, the children at the Clover School had already been using tablets with apps that we had supplied. We were there to better understand how they were being used and also to learn about the community and its needs. We spent the next few days sitting on the floor of a classroom that was previously a one-car garage, watching kids play with apps. When class was over, we would stretch our legs in the courtyard-playground as the kids ran in circles, often stopping to hide behind us, begging us to show them photos of themselves that we had taken with our phones. As the school day ended, we walked through the community to meet and talk with parents and learn about their lives.

There was little to no opportunity for these children to go to a school that would help them become literate. The schools and the government did little to change that. In fact, the system reinforced it. As a result, these parents, children, and, frankly, the whole community, had not believed it possible for their children to learn skills they would need for a better life. Limiting beliefs had taken hold in this community, and they were reinforced by the policies and procedures of the government and the school systems. Our host had managed to break free of these beliefs and bring a whole community of people with her.

———

Visits to places like the Clover School, along with all our conversations over the years with numerous partners and prospective partners, have fueled our process of illuminating limiting beliefs as a first step toward eliminating them. When we travel and engage others with curiosity, we better understand their lives and, with that, their worldviews. We open our eyes to other people's beliefs. As we do this, it is in our nature to compare and contrast their beliefs with our own. The act of doing this allows us to better articulate and understand the beliefs we hold and why we hold them. Seeing our own beliefs is challenging without the reflection that comes from interactions with others—it's like trying to see your face without a mirror.

Mining for Beliefs

The hint that you hold a belief worth investigating often emerges out of conversations with others. That was very much the process for us at Curious Learning. There are moments in conversations within our team or with prospective partners when dialogue starts to shut down. These moments are unlike the natural winding down of a conversation. This shutting-down feeling may involve a member or members of the conversation tuning out. Or someone might say something that brings an abrupt end to a particular line of thought or discussion. These moments are worth noticing; making space for curiosity and attentiveness in these moments often yields insight and deeper understanding.

The best intervention is to start, without judgment, asking questions like—"Would you tell me more about what you're thinking?" "What experiences have you had that might inform this conversation?" "Would you help me understand where that comment or insight comes from?" Or, simply, "Why?" These are the same types of questions you can ask yourself in an internal dialogue. Our experience is that we must be at least willing and, ideally, be able to do this for ourselves to be truly effective when guiding others.

This is a mining process, like digging for gold (see Figure 3). You keep sifting through the material, asking questions, looking for deeper insight, until you find something that can be articulated as a belief. Asking with openness and without judgment is key. Your job at this point is not to evaluate what you are hearing, thinking, or saying. The job is to recognize and articulate the understanding that is guiding the conversation. Then, when you have an idea or insight as to what the belief is, articulate it. Say it or write it down. Look at it for yourself or read it to others and ask them to reflect on it. Understand that the other person is going through

Mining for Beliefs

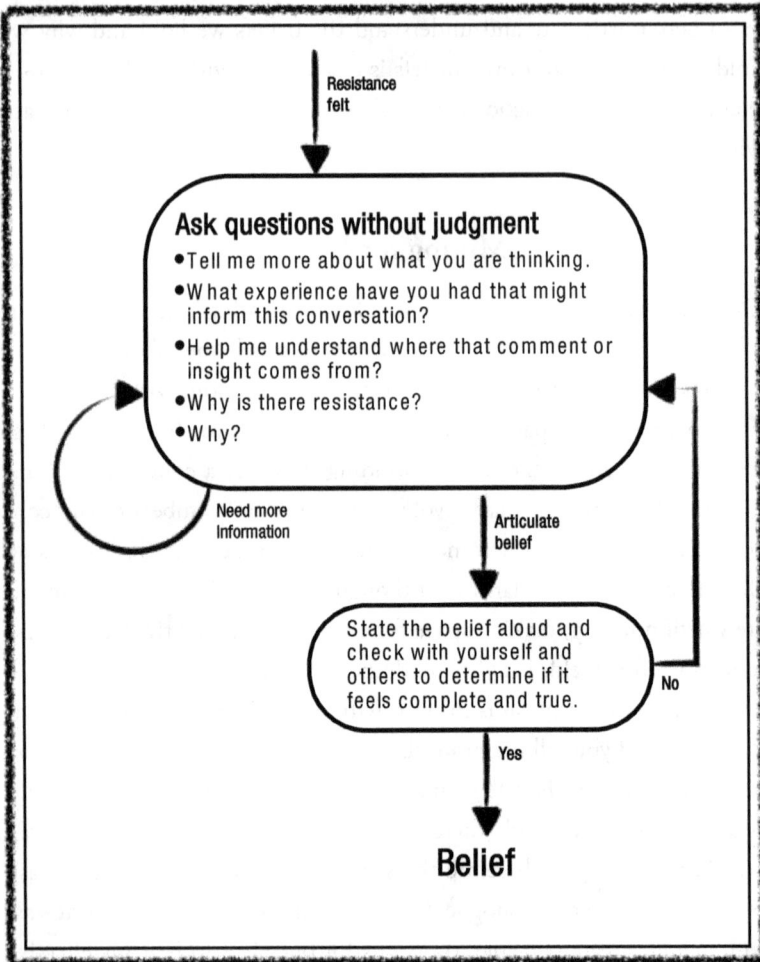

Resistance
felt

Ask questions without judgment
- Tell me more about what you are thinking.
- What experience have you had that might inform this conversation?
- Help me understand where that comment or insight comes from?
- Why is there resistance?
- Why?

Need more
Information

Articulate
belief

State the belief aloud and check with yourself and others to determine if it feels complete and true.

No

Yes

Belief

Figure 3: Diagram outlining the process of Mining for the underlying belief behind resistance to a new idea.

a discovery process as well, and you need to guide each other. The beliefs you are mining for may be buried deeply enough that you might not even be aware of them. Be sensitive to this and supportive of yourself and others in this discovery and applaud the willingness to do this hard work.

For us, this work to articulate our beliefs drew on years of experience, hard work, and self-reflection. It was not a quick process. The nine or so beliefs we are exploring in this book took years to unearth and better understand. One thing I am sure of is the work is not finished and never will be. At some point, we accumulated a clear understanding of at least some of the beliefs that had been governing our thought processes and the conversations we had been having. Then we were ready to reflect upon them. But before jumping into the reflection process, there is one more exercise worth doing.

Stating Goals

This is the step of articulating goals—yours, the organization's, or a larger group's goals. Most people, when asked, can quickly rattle off goals, but rarely are they as simple and concise as they need to be for this process. Here, goals need to be polished and refined, as short and clear as possible. They need to be unencumbered, uncluttered. It is almost always about reducing, editing to arrive at the essence. At Curious Learning, our simple goals are "to reach children and help them learn." Ester's goal could be "to help children prepare for the reading test at age six." Notice that there is no hint of how these goals will be achieved. If you bake the "how" into the goal, you restrict the range of possibilities for how it can be achieved. If you find it difficult to remove the "how" completely, perhaps you are holding onto a belief about how your goal should be achieved. If that is the case, you have uncovered another belief to articulate and write down, another belief to examine. The act of describing this new belief may be the thing that allows you to separate it from your goal.

When analyzing goals, it helps to identify primary goals and goals that serve as stepping stones to primary goals. Take, for example, the goal of getting parents to download literacy apps for their children. For Curious Learning, this is an intermediate goal. It is a stepping stone on the way to the primary goal of reaching children. But it is wrapped up in assumptions and beliefs, like the belief that mobile technology can be used to give everyone the opportunity to learn to read. An intermediate goal may restrict the domain of what is possible. So, beliefs might lurk behind the goal of getting parents to download apps, beliefs that need to be identified, articulated, and examined, so that they don't limit possibilities for realizing the primary goal of reaching children.

Vetting Beliefs

Armed with our newly articulated beliefs and simply stated goals, we are ready to reflect on these beliefs to identify whether or not they are limiting us (see Figure 4). Are they limiting beliefs? We have found three basic questions helpful in this process:

1. Do these beliefs conflict with one another or other beliefs you hold?
2. Do these beliefs inhibit the ability to achieve your goals?
3. Do these beliefs restrict the domain of what is possible?

First, do any two beliefs contradict one another? Place any two beliefs side by side and examine if they are compatible or if they contradict one another. For example, take the belief that "no children left behind" means "an approach is not an acceptable solution unless it works for or reaches everyone." This belief conflicts with other beliefs we may hold, such as "no one approach is going to work in all situations or environments" or "not all learners need the same support." In this case, we experience cognitive dissonance, trying to reconcile two incompatible beliefs. Having found this conflict, the next step is to determine which of the two beliefs is problematic. This problematic or limiting belief can then be examined to see if it still has value and, if so, be adjusted. Take our example of these two beliefs: "An approach is not acceptable unless it works for everyone" and "no one approach works in all situations." In this case, we could correct this conflict by reinterpreting "no child left behind" to mean "we should help those we can now and continue to work to reach everyone." The adjustment or change in the problematic belief brings the two beliefs into compatibility.

Second, does the belief we are vetting conflict with or inhibit our goals? This can be one of the most powerful ways for us to see and adjust limiting beliefs. Once you have articulated, with simplicity, your goals, they become touchstones for thoughts and actions. When you notice something that inhibits these goals, it sticks out like a sore thumb. I would say that this has been the most common way we recognize a limiting belief.

Third, does the belief restrict the set of possible actions you might take to achieve your goals? This process is more nuanced. Take, for example,

Vetting Beliefs

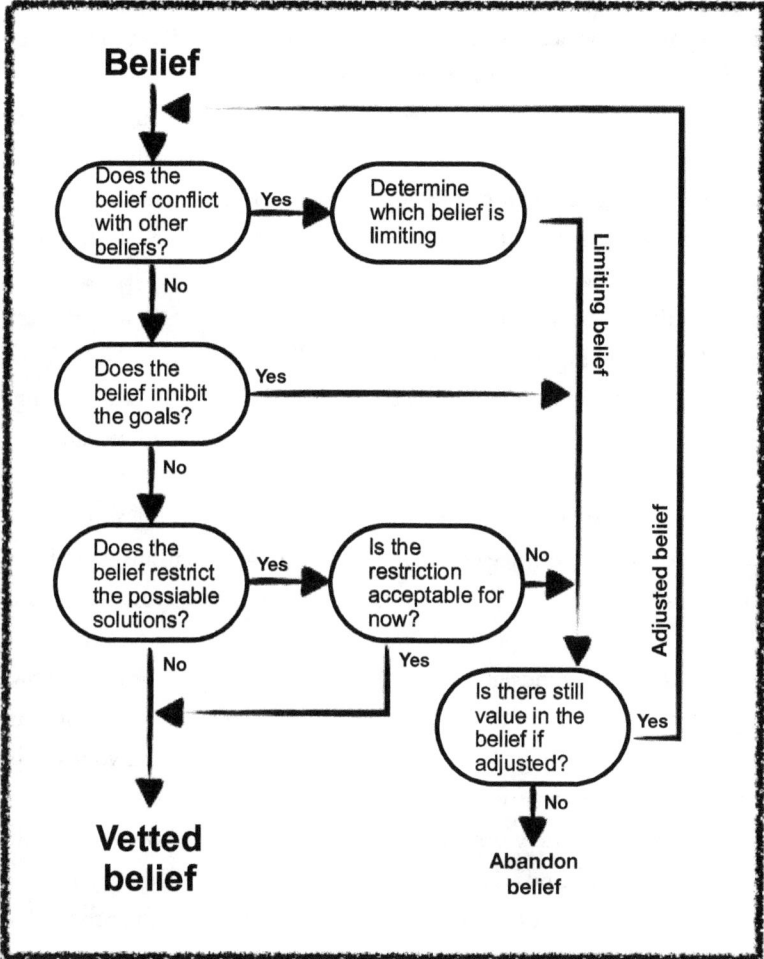

Figure 4: A flow chart that shows a process for vetting a belief by determining if it is a limiting belief and then adjusting it.

the belief that "screen time is bad, especially for children." This belief clearly restricts the domain of possible solutions or actions. The belief that screen time is bad limits our ability to use technology for learning, curtailing the entire field of educational technology. In stark contrast to this belief, we at Curious Learning have embraced the idea that mobile technology can be used to help people learn to read. If we stated that belief as "mobile devices are the way we are going to give everyone the opportunity to learn to read," it would restrict the domain of possible approaches. It closes us down from looking at alternatives that do not include mobile devices. Is this an acceptable restriction? If we make some subtle tweaks to the statement of the belief and acknowledge the restriction that accompanies it, we can mitigate the limitation it may impose in the long run. A new statement of the belief could be "mobile technology can be used to give everyone the opportunity to learn to read." The belief no longer suggests that this is the only approach, and, now, it does support our intended focus.

Examining beliefs is a never-ending process. Our accumulated knowledge and experiences inform the beliefs we hold today. We are always growing and changing, and our beliefs evolve as well. Change is inevitable; this process, therefore, requires revisiting and reevaluating beliefs often.

A wise friend once said something I've never forgotten: "You need to be able to forgive your lesser knowing self." What she meant was, if you look back to any time in your life, you will find decisions you made using the information and experience you had at that moment. Looking back with the clarity of hindsight and scolding your former self for not knowing better is counterproductive. Your past decisions were parts of your learning process; they got you to where you are now. Forgive yourself for not knowing then what you know now.

In that spirit, the work in this book is a statement of where we at Curious Learning find ourselves at this point in time. We, or you, may see flaws or adjustments that need to be made. For now, the process has brought us to a place from which we can take our next steps.

Working with Others and Taking Action

All this analysis of beliefs informs how we will take action to achieve our goals. Taking action generally involves working with others: others in your company or group, partners outside your group, or the people who are affected by your actions. The realization that there are new beliefs to be considered often comes from our interactions with others. For us, conversations with partners, prospective partners, or people using our apps tend to present us with new beliefs. The framework presented below

Working with others and taking action

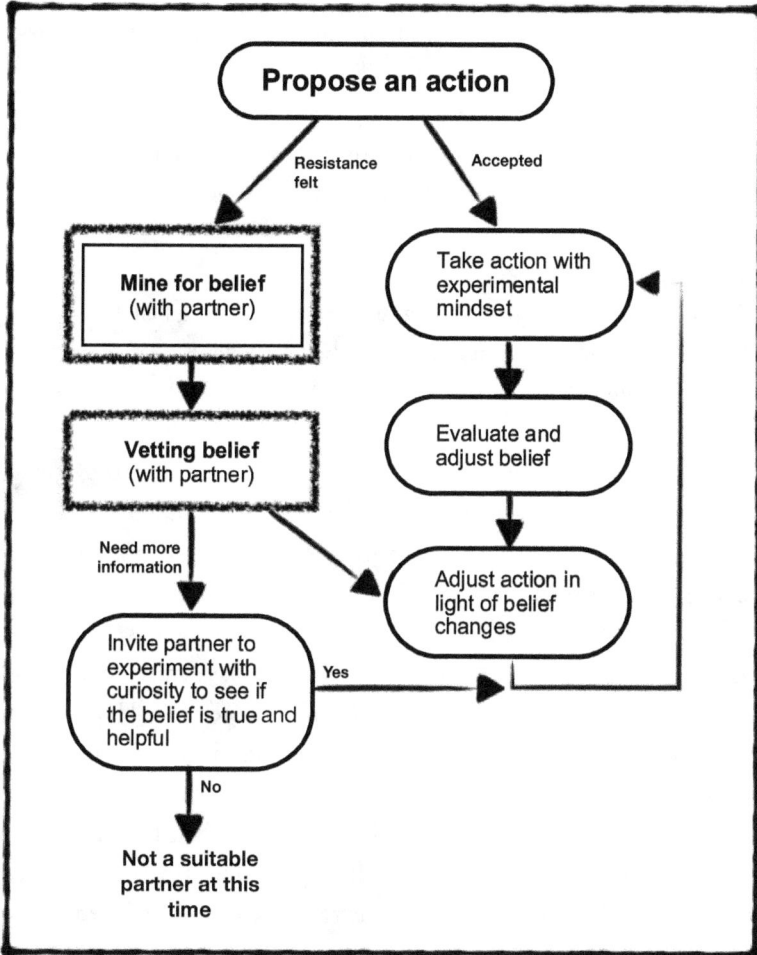

Figure 5: A combined flow chart that uses the process of mining and vetting beliefs to work with others to build consensus and take action.

(see Figure 5) has helped us navigate the processes of both finding and adjusting limiting beliefs and taking action to achieve our goals.

After a conversation to familiarize ourselves with the work, structure, and nature of a potential partner organization, we often find ourselves proposing a course of action. Let's take a conversation we might have with an NGO or ministry of education. We might propose running a short message service (SMS) campaign—a marketing strategy relying on text messages—to promote downloads of an app. This would entail sending a series of text messages to a group of parents over the course of days. These messages would espouse the value of the early literacy apps and encourage parents to download the apps and allow their kids to play with them. After a thorough review of the proposed strategy, our prospective partners will either be excited about the idea or express some resistance. If they accept the proposed action, we proceed with the following cycle:

1. Taking the action
2. Evaluating the results and examining and adjusting beliefs
3. Adjusting the action in light of any belief changes
4. Returning to the first step

This becomes an interactive process, where each iteration provides an opportunity to better achieve goals. If the proposed action meets with resistance, we have more work to do. In nonjudgmental conversation, we need to mine for the belief that is behind the resistance.

Following our example of a proposed SMS campaign, we may learn that the partner believes that most parents don't have smartphones and, even if they did, they would not let their children use them. Having identified these beliefs, we start the process of vetting them with the partner and determining if they are limiting in some way. As always, it is important that we stay open to reevaluating our own beliefs and allowing them to be challenged. When considering limiting beliefs, you always need to start with your own. So, as much as we may believe, based on our experiences and research, that a significant percentage of parents do have smartphones and will let their children use them, we must remain open to the idea that this is not the case for the population this partner wishes to reach. This is a good example of the importance of needing more information to better evaluate the merit of our beliefs.

At this point, through experimentation or research, we and our partners search for additional information to evaluate the value of this belief. Is the belief true or helpful? In this case, how might we assess whether or not parents will download the app and let their children play with it? It is easy to suggest an experiment to gather this information. We might propose a pilot where we run a small campaign for a few schools or a district and examine the data. From this action, we can directly measure how many downloads we get and how much the apps are used. If our partners are amenable to this, we can actively begin our interactive experimental process. If the partner is resistant, we return to the search for other beliefs that might be informing their resistance. In some cases, digging for beliefs can become cumbersome or uncomfortable, which may prove to be counterproductive. Ultimately, it may be better to step back, recognizing that this partnership might not be workable for the time being. This does not mean, however, that it won't be in the future, as all parties and situations evolve and change over time.

This example demonstrates the value and importance of encouraging and maintaining an experimental mindset. Staying curious and open to new information fuels the progression of the work and the evolution of our own belief systems, becoming an engine that is constantly discovering limiting beliefs and transcending them.

As we have evolved and applied this process over the past years, we have identified nine limiting beliefs related to our work. The table below (see Figure 6) lists these beliefs chapter by chapter alongside alternative beliefs that free us from limitations, at least the limitations we are able to see for now.

———

Back in Kampala, we sat on the floor of the classroom with the garage door open to a beautiful sunny day. The children sat on the floor playing with the apps on tablets. You can never anticipate what children will do when left to their own devices; this always surprises me. Here, the kids were interacting with an app that played a short song when they made a series of mistakes. The song was intended to indicate an incorrect action. Six kids had all gathered together and had this app open. They carefully watched each other to make sure they were touching the screen in unison. Having navigated to the moment where the "error" song plays, they all triggered it at the same time, then stood up and danced together. They certainly were not limited by some set of beliefs of how the apps should or should not be used. These children showed us that they were not born with limiting beliefs, and they were still too young to have acquired them from family and social conditioning.

LIMITING BELIEFS	ALTERNATIVE BELIEFS
No Child Left Behind	
It is not an acceptable solution unless it works for everyone.	We should help those we can now and continue to work to reach everyone.
Learning to Read	
Learning to read is easy; all one needs is books.	Although learning to read is difficult, there are a set of skills that can be cultivated to facilitate reading.
The Power of a New Medium	
Screen time is bad, especially for children.	Technology is a tool that can be used for positive change.
Children all over the world should be given only "the best."	We need to try things to better understand what best helps different people.
Curriculum Conundrum	
Anything we do needs to be consistent with the curriculum.	We want to develop new, effective ways to educate children.
Illiteracy Is Never an Emergency	
Illiteracy is not life-threatening, so it need not be a priority.	The ability to read is linked to not just surviving but thriving, so it should be a priority.
Reframing Sustainability	
Nonprofit missions are best served by the nonprofit being financially sustainable.	By focusing first on a nonprofit's mission, we may find new ways to realize that mission that provide a different definition of sustainable.
Relearning Curiosity	
Failure marks a stopping point in the educational process.	By being curious, failure is redefined as a necessary and informative part of the learning process.
Educational opportunities are for those who meet the conditions of admission.	Everyone deserves access to equitable quality education.

Figure 6: Table of limiting beliefs and a proposed alternative that does not harbor the same limitations from throughout the book.

As the tablet time ended, we stretched our legs and joined one of the staff members who had offered to introduce us to some of the parents and serve as our translator as we followed the children on their walk home. It was a quasi-rural community on the edge of the city. We walked past a woman sitting on the side of the dirt path beside her box of various vegetables for sale. The dirt was a red clay, apparently well-suited (or at least good enough) for making bricks. I watched a man repeatedly dig up the clay and mash it into a small wooden box to form it into a brick. He would turn the box over and, with a smack, add its contents to the ever-growing row of bricks on the hillside set out to dry in the sun.

One of the boys walking home from school with us ran ahead as we got close to his home to greet his mother. She was sitting on the ground outside. The entire family lived in a dirt-floored, one-room structure that was a little smaller than a one-car garage. She was cooking on her charcoal stove that was about the size and shape of a flowerpot (also made of clay). She had a fire going in the bottom and a rack on top holding a dented pot that contained some sort of stew. There was no running water, and, as is often the case in these informal settlements, the latrine was a cesspit at the end of a row of one-room homes.

Our guide and translator introduced us and let the mom know we were there to better understand how the tablets were working and if the children were learning by using them. She excitedly talked about how her son would come home to tell her all about the tablets and apps he was playing with. She told us that he had started to teach the alphabet to his younger brother the way the app had taught him. These people were certainly living with more limitations than most of us can imagine. But the Clover School, that house-turned-into-a-school, and the lovely work Ester Makumbi was doing had clearly helped the people living in these small homes experience what was possible.

When Ester decided to turn her house into a school, she shed so many beliefs that would have encumbered most of us: These people can't learn. The system is stacked against them. My house is not a school. She, in turn, empowered this mother to shed some of her limiting beliefs: I have no options. No one cares. My children can't learn. I can't afford school. Our host had felt a call to service that was greater than herself, and she had answered it. She was able to because she did not let perceived limitations get in her way.

———

There is a strong and powerful global intention to provide everyone with opportunities to learn. Our work to bring new ways for people to learn to read into reality is fueled by this intention. We work to take action ourselves and cultivate actions in others that allow this intention to physically manifest on earth. We are working to be a grounding agent for this intention.

A significant part of our work is the facilitation of discussions around beliefs that we hold as individuals and as societies, beliefs that play a role in our ability to realize the goals of this intention around education. Shifting these beliefs is an essential part of our ability to succeed. For those of us working in social development, shifting our relationships with our beliefs alone will effect more significant change than any one action or program we might institute. When we shift our beliefs, we become beacons for others. Others see, hear, and feel how differently we are working and become inspired to try new approaches themselves. Being vulnerable, self-reflective, and willing to take risks may serve as a kind of permission for others to do the same, encouraging them to expand their understanding of what is possible. The broader and deeper this shift in perception, the greater the potential for a global shift that will allow us as a global society to take the next best steps in transcending self-imposed limitations. By engaging in this process, we as individuals facilitate our own learning and growth in service of facilitating the learning and growth of all.

Embracing Transformation

A World Based on Learning and Growing

Pandemic Pandemonium

By the end of November 2021, I had been in Durban, South Africa, for about a week. With all the travel that had been canceled due to the pandemic over the previous couple of years, this was a welcome opportunity to be working in person again. We finished our first week of testing our latest work with children and were gearing up to start a second week. Then the announcement came.

South African epidemiologists, many of them in Durban, had run one of the best, if not *the best*, variant surveillance programs in the world. They had had years of experience following AIDS and Ebola on the African continent, and they were putting their knowledge and resources to work tracking COVID. They announced the discovery of the Omicron variant.

The world responded so quickly and extensively that the plans for our little group must have changed at least five or six times in a matter of only forty-eight hours. European countries started to enact restrictions that prevented people from entering their countries if coming from South Africa. Our European partners were rightfully concerned about being stuck in South Africa, so they quickly jumped on flights home. When the dust settled, our team of eight people had dwindled to three.

The irony of all this was that the South African epidemiologists had been clear that they did not know the origin of Omicron and needed samples from other countries to be sequenced to determine the origin. Their suspicion was that Omicron was already in many countries, and they were right; Omicron had arrived in Africa via Belgian diplomats. Why Europe responded so quickly without having all the facts when a new variant was announced in Africa is unclear. They had not responded with the same vigor when earlier variants were discovered in high-income countries. I suspect a limiting belief was at work.

As the conversation continued, the name Omicron quickly became shortened to "Om." The craziness that this syllable induced in the world contrasted sharply with my experiences of chanting the same syllable during meditation and yoga practice—Om as inducer of anxiety versus Om as sacred sound that quiets the mind.

The experience was another stark reminder of how the disruption of the pandemic had rippled through everyone's lives. In relation to Curious Learning's work, that wave was upending education.

By the end of 2022, data were suggesting that the number of children reading for meaning in sub-Saharan Africa had dropped from 12 percent to only 10 percent, and in India, from 20 percent to 15 percent. And this was only the beginning of the impact.

The waves of change that the pandemic created would continue to ripple through for years to come. We stood on the precipice of losing nearly an entire generation to illiteracy. The pandemic disrupted the education of the youngest learners the most, those at the beginning or in the process of learning to read. Curious Learning's work had thus become even more relevant. Our conversations with prospective partners expanded, our programs with partners expanded, and opportunities to share what we had learned and to guide transformation expanded. Due to the pandemic, more doors have opened to our work than closed. Every crisis creates an opportunity for transformation—maybe Om is a reminder of that opportunity.

Thinking Differently and Letting Go of Victimhood

The pandemic was hugely disruptive to many aspects of life. The disruption to education was a big part of what transpired. Disruptions like this tend to knock us out of our ruts and force us to think differently. A simple example of this was the use of devices with screens for education. Before the pandemic, I had many conversations about our work where the idea that screen time is bad for children came up. This idea or belief was often incomplete and out of context. Regardless, there was a belief wrapped in fear that screen time of any type was bad for children. As schools shut down and so much learning went online, these concerns went out the window. That limiting belief was disrupted and discarded. Disruption can be fertile ground for shifting beliefs and, with them, behaviors.

Every one of us, at some point, felt we were victims of the pandemic. We were victims of having our daily lives disrupted and, with that, our social time, our work, our education, and our physical and mental health. But there's always another way to look at the world. Every event, no matter how dire, is an opportunity or, better yet, an invitation to think differently. In the case of education, the pandemic invited us to explore how new technologies could be used, how online resources could foment learning, how personal curiosity could be activated and satisfied, and how departure from traditional curricula could provide new pathways for learning.

Over the years, I have actively worked to shift my thoughts away from victimhood and toward the opportunities that any new situation provides. This simple shift in thinking grants me the freedom to look at things from a different perspective. When I do this, doors open and light pours in. The dark veils of victimhood are lifted, and the excitement of what is possible starts to bubble up. Alternatives that I would otherwise never have contemplated present themselves. I shift from the stagnation of victimhood to the enlivening energy of learning and growing. The more I embrace even the simplest of events that irritate me in my everyday life, the more the magic of the universe reveals itself to me.

There is a grace to how the universe constantly pushes up against our most entrenched limiting beliefs, reminding us to pay attention to them. We only need to be open to the universe's messages and listen to them. Being open and listening are among the simplest and hardest things we must do in our lives. In the moments when we manage to achieve this kind of attentiveness, we arrive in flow with ourselves and others. Here, we find joy that needs no external validation, for we feel the support of the entire universe surrounding us. Each one of these moments recharges us and prepares us to step into the next cycle, the next event that challenges us to resist victimhood in favor of responding receptively, open to thinking differently.

To survive, our basic needs must be met. Organizations work hard globally, helping the most impoverished among us to meet the basic needs of food, clothing, and shelter. Once basic needs are met, space opens, allowing people to view their lives differently. But seeing differently isn't sufficient; people need to find their own power, acquiring skills for self-advocacy and resources for satisfying their own basic needs. Education is the most powerful tool for enabling self-empowerment, and the foundation of education is literacy. Other programs in development are starting to understand this. Successful programs that address food security, child labor, human trafficking, infant mortality, and other crucial issues are finding that as soon as their programs slow down, the problems they were addressing reemerge unless education is also addressed. Education affords people the skills to manage these needs for themselves. As the familiar adage instructs, "Give a person a fish, and they will eat for a day; teach them to fish, and they will eat for a lifetime."

The traditional models of working in low- and middle-income countries for almost every NGO and multilateral organization are focused on the most impoverished, those undoubtedly with the greatest need. In the countries most targeted by these organizations, there are two confounding facts when it comes to addressing the education crisis. First, only about 10 to15 percent of children in these countries read at grade level. Second, the 25 to 35 percent living in extreme poverty are often the hardest to reach. Conventional wisdom is to focus on the bottom of the poverty pyramid, because this is where we find the most desperate victims. By focusing on only the most impoverished to the exclusion of others, a middle 60+ percent are not being helped.

With respect to Curious Learning's mission, we did not need to look very hard at the pandemic to see a new way of thinking about giving everyone the opportunity to learn to read. What if we thought of illiteracy as an epidemic and the act of learning to read as a vaccine? How would this way of thinking change our approach? With this reframing, our job became to vaccinate the world against illiteracy. How do we do that? We give everyone the opportunity to learn to read. Because it is rare for a literate parent to raise an illiterate child, this becomes a vaccination that carries into future generations.

In high-income countries, the majority of the population is already vaccinated. Sure, there are plenty of arguments about how even in the United States we should be doing better; but, for the most part, we have a kind of herd immunity when it comes to literacy. Looking at low-income and some medium-income countries, where the need for the vaccination is largest, we can break the populations into three categories. First, those who are already immune: They have a literate parent and will receive the resources they need to learn to read. This covers about 10 to 15 percent of the population. Second, those who are easy to reach: With our approach, they have access to a smartphone but are unlikely to become sufficiently literate. This group includes about 40 to 60 percent of the population and is rapidly growing to 75 percent or more most everywhere. What we are left with are, third, those who are hard to reach but who desperately need the vaccine to pull themselves out of poverty. This covers roughly 15 to 20 percent of the population.

We have two big advantages over traditional vaccines. First, the infrastructure—the devices and bandwidth needed to deliver the vaccine—already exists and is expanding in size and capability due to market demands. Second, the vaccine is free and free to replicate. This vaccine is a simple piece of software (an app) that can be digitally replicated for little to no cost. We get to skip the manufacturing and shipping process. But we still need the awareness and adoption process.

So how do we start? What is the most efficient way to vaccinate the world? If you want to make rapid progress, you don't start with the hardest to reach people first. You start with those who are easiest to reach: those parents who already have smartphones, those parents who actively seek opportunities for their children to learn to read, and those parents who only need to hear about it once and they will download an app and give their phone to their child. This approach targets the middle population, the largest portion of the population, the 70+ percent who have a smartphone but are unlikely to learn to read. While, arguably, some percentage of this population will have limiting beliefs that prevent them from valuing the potential literacy of their children, this is only a subset of this population. As with a medical vaccine, it all depends on getting to the people you can right away. Reaching them creates the opportunity to reach others over time. As an individual who is reluctant to get vaccinated, the fact that more of your community becomes vaccinated (learning to read) may shift your willingness to get vaccinated or vaccinate your children.

As the vaccinated percentage of a country's population grows, everyone is lifted: social and cultural norms shift, economic growth jumps, and more resources become available for everyone. We are simultaneously treating the individual with a vaccine and the global whole as an inter-connected planetary organism. We start building herd immunity against illiteracy. This is the power of an epidemiological approach. We are lever-aging the fact that people everywhere are interconnected. The health of individuals eventually results in the health of the entire population. This is a new and fundamentally different approach to education.

Just Try Things

At Curious Learning, we believe that we have to try things in order to learn. This is foundational and grows out of our roots in research. What would happen if we were to give kids apps? Could they learn to read? Would other kids in other places and circumstances also learn? Which apps most engage children? Which apps and activities have the most learning impact? The list goes on. Every question we answer opens us to new questions. We see this as a never-ending learning and improvement cycle that has the advantage of allowing us to adapt continuously. We don't allow the "perfect" to get in the way of the "good."

The 2019 World Bank study in northern Nigeria showed us how much children engage with and learn from Feed the Monster when they have access to it. For those versed in statistics, the intervention yielded a 0.5 change in standard deviation within months. What that means in this region of northern Nigeria is that the children learned in months what they would have only learned in 4.9 years in school. That says as much about how poor the schools are as how good the intervention was. This is a big improvement that happened fast.

These results also provoked the next question: Can we take advantage of the massive expansion of smartphones and get parents to download apps and give them to their kids? We could have easily said to ourselves that we didn't think that would happen—that people who are poorer than we are would not dare give their phones to their kids as we do. But that would have been adopting a belief for which we did not have evidence and making assumptions about what people unlike us would or would not do. If we had adopted that limiting belief, we would never have reached 130,000 kids in Nepal in four months or a similar number in Ukraine in the middle of a war. We wouldn't have spent US$188 to reach 17,000 kids in Afghanistan, where, data suggest, at least 46 percent of those kids were girls.

You don't need to have all the answers when you start, but you do need to start, and you need to try many things to learn and build evidence. You can't let conventional wisdom or personal suspicions stop you from trying new things. So, we try things, we collect data, and we learn in an effort to figure out the next best step and the right questions to ask.

We have started the process of embedding games in the apps that assess a child's literacy skills. In this way, our distribution model merges with our research model, a power that only technology provides. Large tech companies use these approaches every day to study how they can get more money out of consumers—why not learn from that and use the same infrastructure to optimize learning? As we get to scale, the hope is this engine will rev up and the data it produces will enable all kinds of research and insights.

Learning to read is considered a basic human right. Ideally, everyone in the world should be given an equal opportunity to build basic literacy skills. As we all know, this is not the current state of the world. Curious Learning's goal is to see the end of global illiteracy in our lifetime. With this in mind, Curious Learning goes to great lengths to understand and utilize the science behind learning to read in order to create digital learning tools that are not only available to anyone anywhere in the world but that cater to the ways the human brain learns.

However, it is important to remember that beyond science, every learner is a unique person, both on an individual level and at the population level. Each individual learner, as well as each community, faces different challenges when it comes to learning to read. The goal of Curious Learning is not to replace current teaching methods; instead, its goal is to provide opportunity and access in places where those traditional methods are not readily available or would take too long to implement in light of the current learning crisis the world is facing. The beauty of this approach is that it can supplement traditional approaches, like schools and teacher training. We believe that the key to eradicating global illiteracy is not only providing a new resource for learners everywhere but also filling in the gaps in populations where any kind of educational access or success is scarce.

Not every type of learning or educational resource works for everyone, whether the obstacle they face is individual or systemic to the community in which they live. This is where we remind ourselves of the difference between equality and equity. Equality is giving everyone the same thing. Equity is giving individuals what they need in an effort to raise everyone to the same level. By pushing to provide everyone around the world with the exact same type of educational resource (i.e., schools) without providing additional resources in places where schools are currently unavailable or underperforming, we are actively choosing to hold back literacy learning opportunities from millions of learners. However, if we can provide an ever-growing and improving set of digital learning tools to children everywhere, then we open the door for each learner to reach their full educational potential.

Through our work, Curious Learning has found that the best way to refine this approach is to learn as we go. We take our best guess at how to provide learning experiences to communities as a conduit to our own learning. We are not telling people how to learn; we are helping people to tell us how they learn best. With the data that our apps collect, we are able to learn directly from millions of learners worldwide what works best and use that knowledge to improve our methods. I have said this before, the name Curious Learning was chosen for its double meaning: to not only activate the curiosity of the learner but also to support our own curiosity about how children will learn.

Nothing Can Be Done Alone

I fundamentally believe that the world is in a learning crisis, and literacy learning is foundational. Without restating all the statistics, I will simply state that it is time for an all-hands-on-deck approach. The longer it takes to address this crisis, the more children slip through the cracks, and the more people suffer. This problem is so large and so daunting that it would be irresponsible to think that only one approach is needed.

We, as a world, have to come together to solve this problem, with many people and groups trying many different things—a tapestry of projects and approaches. This learning crisis requires a range of actions, like the work that is happening to create an innovative teacher training program in isiXhosa (one of the eleven official South African languages), to repeatedly developing and testing programs that leverage the massive infrastructure that the smartphone and wireless carrier industry is creating across the full economic breadth of society. To fill this canvas, it is going to take a combination of the broad brushstrokes of Curious Learning and the precise lines of the numerous NGOs working tirelessly within their communities, along with a host of other techniques and approaches.

I have come to believe that we need the help of others for everything we do. In Buddhist philosophy, this is the concept of interconnectedness. The classic example to illustrate this is to look at an object in your life. Take a chair in your house, maybe even the one you are sitting on right now. Think about what and who it took to make that chair available to you: the store clerk who sold it to you, the truck driver who delivered it, the upholsterer who covered it, the woodworker who constructed the frame, the factory worker who made the screws, the power-plant worker who helped generate the electricity needed, and the engineers who designed the power plant. The list goes on forever. Eventually, you will have listed most of the people currently on the planet, as well as those from the past. You can do that same exercise with anything in your life. I find it particularly poignant to do this exercise with something you need for survival, like the food you eat. When you follow this thought process to its natural conclusion, you realize everyone needs everyone else to live and have their needs met.

For those of us who pride ourselves on our ability to take care of ourselves, this may seem disempowering. But as we lean into this notion of interconnected unity, we actually discover great joy and a new kind of power. We stop seeing others as competitors, and we start seeing everyone as collaborators, even if they don't see us in the same way. What is possible exponentially expands as we embrace the realization that we are always in collaboration with everyone else.

Grateful for Those Who Came Before Us

In many ways, our collaboration extends back in time, for we owe a debt of gratitude to all those who came before us. In our case, literacy education is an issue that pretty much every school and government has wrestled with for decades or centuries. I visualize these many different ways of providing literacy education as a landscape, a landscape that is still being surveyed and mapped. Many parts of this landscape have been well-traveled and are well-known, parts like the building of schools, the training of teachers, and a variety of different curricula. These are important parts of the landscape, but they are not the whole thing. There is more to explore.

So, to those explorers who came before us, we raise a glass, and we thank them for traveling what was then unknown territory. We thank them for their struggles, which revealed problematic paths, and for their successes, which highlighted actions worth incorporating or adapting. Their exploration exposed areas that may at one time have been quite helpful and productive but have now become depleted and less relevant to us today.

Most importantly, the pathfinders who preceded us show us the areas that have not been traveled and that remain, as yet, unmapped. As we become explorers, we step into these new landscapes. To do this successfully, we need to maintain an experimental mindset, allowing ourselves to try things, to forge paths on new ground, and to discover if this new ground is worth traveling, worth mapping. We need to be cartographers, never blaming ourselves for going the wrong way—there is no wrong way on this adventure. We must always be forgiving of our lesser-knowing selves, always honoring them.

Once we have learned all there is to learn from taking one path, it is time to try another, to move on. Holding tight to any process or belief beyond its usefulness is counterproductive; it is succumbing to limiting beliefs. When we find a more fruitful path, we stand up and call out to others, pointing the way to something worth seeing on that far horizon. We share what we have discovered and illustrate what is newly possible. We are filling in a new part of the map to share with the world.

Help Is Always There

In February 2023, I was awakened at 5:00 a.m. by the sound of a mosquito buzzing in my ear—surprisingly, not an uncommon occurrence in South Africa, as it seems screens are not a thing on this continent. After several attempts to facilitate the mosquito's transition into its next incarnation, I started to drift off.

As I surfed the edge between being awake and being asleep, I tipped into a dreamscape. I stood, looking at an open field on the edge of a road. In the distance was a cabin, a shack of sorts, that reminded me of some of the old wooden structures you might find in the hills of West Virginia, where I grew up. These were structures built before there were many roads. They, more often than not, were a short (sometimes a long) hike from the edge of a road. This cabin had a small falling-apart front porch; for that matter, the whole thing was kind of falling apart. A child stood on that porch, staring blank-eyed in my direction. To the right of the porch was a barren tree that appeared near dead. The field between the boy on the porch and me reminded me of fields in Cambodia off the sides of roads. As a visitor to Cambodia, I was warned not to walk through these areas; they were often littered with unexploded landmines left behind by the Khmer Rouge. The poignancy of this warning was punctuated by the number of locals you would see with missing limbs. There was no doubt in my mind that this field in my dream was indeed a minefield.

As I slowly and carefully moved toward the boy and the shack, I had an innate sense of where and where not to step to avoid the landmines. I was moving thoughtfully but also without fear. Eventually, I came to a place where the mines could not be sidestepped. I stopped to consider my options. Much to my surprise, I looked up to find I had a companion, a person who had just the right tools to disarm the landmines and clear a path. We proceeded together, methodically and competently. Every time I felt stuck, my companion was there to provide exactly what I needed to proceed.

Before long, we were halfway to the shack, and I stopped to take in our progress and surroundings. What had previously appeared in sepia, almost black and white, had now taken on the hyper-real colors of a digitally enhanced picture: green leaves and white blossoms on the tree, a red shirt on the boy who had returned to play, skipping in an improvised dance of unleashed joy. Though we had not yet reached the porch, I felt a connection with this one child, satisfied in an awareness that I had helped him from a distance. The feeling of accomplishment and insight brought the dream to a natural transition. I awakened as the imagery before me faded.

Our work at Curious Learning is all about reaching children in need, who would otherwise not have the opportunity to learn to read, and giving them that opportunity. The path to succeeding in this work is littered with the landmines of limiting beliefs. I, and, more broadly, Curious Learning, have been navigating and will continue to navigate these limiting beliefs. Trusted companions always walk beside us, ready to help us change those limiting beliefs when needed. Help will come in other forms, too. The children themselves will use the apps and show adults in their lives what is possible. The data and insights that flow back to us at Curious Learning will help expose and remove any limiting beliefs we hold. The parents who take that leap of faith to download the apps and make them available to their children will help. And you, reader, are helping by reading this book and contemplating our story. Together, may we all do our best to remain open and curious and willing to take action to transform limiting beliefs.

Help with recognizing and deactivating limiting beliefs is the most important kind of support we can ask for as an organization. As wonderful as it is to reach every new child, it is the change in belief systems that will have the largest, most sustained impact on the world. No one and everyone can be credited for that change.

The most important kind of help one can receive as an individual is help with illuminating and changing one's own limiting beliefs, which is the journey of living and growing. The magical universe is always there to help us. Change is not always comfortable, and help isn't always visible, but we can take comfort in knowing it is always there. Every uncomfortable event in our lives, every time we fall into the trap of seeing ourselves as a victim of circumstances is a kind of help. In these moments, we can stop and reflect and wonder if our beliefs are still serving us and our goals. Help is always there, just not always in a form that we recognize without deep personal reflection.

———

I have noticed in my travels that people living with fewer resources often seem more in touch with the notion that help is always there. In the first years of the Curious Learning journey, I was asked to go to Peru to meet with a group that was starting to use mobile devices in rural classrooms.

After arriving in Lima, my host, Brian O'Hara (yes, he is Peruvian despite bearing the name of an Irishman), and I jumped on a flight to Cusco. From there we took a series of daytrips up into the mountains to visit several schools. The day started with a walk across Cusco to a bus stop, then an hour's ride on a winding road down a steep hillside that brought us to a small town on the edge of a lovely, fast-moving river. This town was known for growing a type of quinoa that has a particularly high nutritional value. Apparently, NASA's interest in this quinoa as a food source for their astronauts had created a small economic boom for the region. This town was a waypoint before we reached the schools we had planned to visit.

We had reached the limits of the bus system. As always seems to happen, need breeds ingenuity. An old car pulled up, and, following Brian's lead, we climbed in. A few locals with cars had taken it upon themselves to create a quasi-taxi service. They drove around the region looking for people who needed rides and picked them up for a small fee. As we proceeded, the driver would stop to pick up and drop off others. At one point, an elderly woman climbed in through the rear door of the hatchback and sat on the floor. I considered offering her my seat until I realized she would never accept the offer—riding in the back was less expensive. Not long after she got in the car, I heard a kitten meow and poke its head out of her jacket. She had come in closer to town to pick up this kitten. She had a mouse problem at home—they were making away with her grain stores.

After dropping the woman and her kitten, we reached our destination, now only a short walk to the school. Cusco is over 11,000 feet above sea level, and we had been going mostly up all day. The clear, sunny day and high altitude made for long, beautiful views. The school was small, only a couple dozen students, and mostly open air with a classroom and one or two other small rooms. A powerline that looked more like an extension cord hung on small poles made its way to one of the smaller rooms. This had been installed as a way to charge their mobile devices. For as little as they had, they were not lacking in abundant natural beauty, which surrounded them.

After a lovely visit and discussion about how these devices could best help the students, we headed out. Brian said, "Let's walk." After we reached the crest of the rise and were looking down toward a number of small clusters of buildings, I asked how we would get back. In a calming tone, Brian said, "They'll find us."

We wandered where our curiosity led us. This area had a population of ceramics artisans. We passed houses surrounded by boards laid out on the ground covered with handmade objects drying in the sun: cups, statues, bowls, plates. We walked among locals shepherding goats or sheep from one place to another. Everyone turned our way at least long enough to offer a welcoming nod. As predicted, a car eventually pulled up behind us and the driver asked if we needed a ride. For a community that had so few resources by our standards, there was always a friendly face, and I had no doubt any of them would have helped in whatever way was needed.

These people, like those in the many impoverished communities I have had the privilege of visiting over the years, rarely saw themselves as victims of their circumstances. They had daily needs and issues, and they got on with addressing them. They helped others and they received the help they needed. I sometimes think that the more we have, the more isolated we become. And the more isolated we become, the more we forget that we live in an interconnected world, where helping one another is a given. I believe the universe is always placing help before us—we need only look up long enough to notice and accept it.

As I was finishing this manuscript, I was struggling to think of a story to help illustrate this last point. After racking my brain, I did what I often do, which is set it aside and wait. As I picked up my phone, I found a message that had come in out of the blue from Brian O'Hara. We had not talked for a couple of years, and hearing from him was a welcome surprise. I stopped to reflect on our time together and realized this was the story.

Appendix

Reflecting on the simple goals of reaching children and helping them learn to read naturally leads to examining the more complicated area of those beliefs that guide us. This kind of examination can reveal areas of potential growth and areas of stagnation. Which of our beliefs support the goals of reaching and learning? Which beliefs inhibit and restrict us? Awareness of the difference can liberate us from limiting beliefs, allowing us to reframe them, while remaining open, curious, creative, and aligned with our goals. Below is an analysis of some of the beliefs that have surfaced in earlier chapters.

Belief: **It is not an acceptable solution unless it works for everyone.**
Chapter: No Child Left Behind

Any approach that works for everyone is a kind of one-size-fits-all approach. These kinds of approaches leave no room for trying things that effectively reach just a segment of a population, which can be a great start. A requirement that any solution must work for all tends to create delays and inhibit action, while solutions with a smaller impact can be more nimble and lead to multiple, more broad-reaching solutions. All exploration and experimentation tend to stop when faced with the need to find a single approach that reaches everyone. The belief that it is necessary to reach all puts on hold the opportunity to help those you can reach. Simply put, this belief inhibits the ability to reach children.

Likewise with learning. This belief suggests that you must have an approach that will allow everyone to learn. Yet research shows that not everyone will learn from the same material. So a one-size-fits-all approach is destined to deprive some children of learning. Therefore, a series of different approaches, or variations on approaches, is necessary to enable everyone to learn. Some solutions will help some but not others, which is better than helping none. This belief inhibits the use of such solutions, requiring instead that we have a full complement of solutions to enable everyone to learn before we deploy any one specific solution.

While the original intent behind this belief, to help everyone, is noble, it would benefit from some adjustment so that it does not serve as a barrier to reaching children and allowing them to learn.

Belief: *Learning to read is easy; all one needs is books.*
Chapter: Learning to Read

Books have been around for a long time. We know how to print and deliver them. From the standpoint of reaching children, giving out books is of great help and has the potential to reach everyone. So this belief actually helps the goal of reaching all children.

From a learning perspective, though, data show that only about 10 to15 percent of the population can learn to read with exposure to text in a literacy-rich environment. Books alone do not create a literacy-rich environment. In addition, most of the population requires structure, which assures that all the skills needed for reading are supported. Getting appropriate books into the hands of children is never a bad thing, but believing that this task is all that is needed for learning to read is misguided. Learning to read is more complicated than just shipping out books.

Belief: *Screen time is bad, especially for children.*
Chapter: The Power of a New Medium

Inherent in the belief that screen time is bad for children is the idea that we should limit the amount of time that children spend on devices with screens. But, does restricting or abolishing screen time help our goal of reaching children with literacy interventions? Mobile devices are proliferating at a rate that is unparalleled. This technology is ending up in the hands of more and more people every day. Screens are one of the most effective ways to reach people in general. Believing that screen time is inherently bad for children obscures the reality that screens are often the best way to reach children. Considering how children are using their screens opens a possibility for reframing this belief.

Belief: **Children all over the world should be given only *"the best."***
Chapter: The Power of a New Medium

In our context, "the best" means the best educational material and opportunities, in particular the best smartphones and apps. For a middle-income American, the best smartphone may cost US$600; for a day laborer in a low-income country, who makes US$2 a day, the best smartphone may cost only US$35. So, setting aside which idea of "the best" is used as a measure, the notion of restricting what can be implemented only to "the best" is just that, a restriction. This belief limits who can be reached.

Applying this belief to "the best" apps is a little more nuanced. In the context of apps, does "the best" imply best design? Most complete educational material? Most engaging to children? For our purposes, we might define "the best" apps as those that most engage children and best promote the most learning. Others will have their own criteria for defining "the best" app. Is there a way to build a more objective measure? Ideally, any objective measure would allow different apps to be "better" choices for different populations, in support of that population's learning. So it would appear this belief would benefit from some modification.

Belief: **Anything we do needs to be consistent with the curriculum.**
Chapter: Curriculum Conundrum

In the context of this belief, any new approach to learning that is not deemed to be aligned with a curriculum would be immediately dismissed by the educational system. This belief rests on the idea that the currently determined curriculum is an appropriate measure of whether new learning material should be considered. Therefore, it restricts the exploration of any new pedagogy or educational material that falls outside the current definition of curriculum. In this way, this belief restricts opportunities for new approaches (even those that have research evidence showing their learning effectiveness) from reaching students via a school system. This may have been a helpful paradigm when there was no easy way to evaluate the effectiveness of a new approach. In the context of new technologies, there is the opportunity to build new criteria for judging whether learning is happening. This would open or remove the limits this belief places on what is possible.

It is also worth remembering that only 12 percent of children are reading at grade level by fourth grade in sub-Saharan Africa. This means that something in the current system is not facilitating learning. The curriculum itself is potentially an impediment.

Belief: **Illiteracy is not life threatening, so it need not be a priority.**
Chapter: Illiteracy Is Never an Emergency

It is hard to argue with this statement. When you don't have food, or you are on your deathbed needing medical care, your priority is not learning to read. A problem arises when more urgent needs end up excluding literacy learning as a priority altogether. But most development programs that address issues involving threats to life report the positive impact education has on their programs. Supporting the development of new skills in a population, especially through education, provides tools people need to actively engage in addressing their own most urgent concerns. So, if we keep only prioritizing threats to life, we end up endlessly plugging holes in the dike, never reconstructing it so that it no longer leaks. Reaching children with literacy interventions could transform their lives, equipping them to eventually solve problems for their communities and for future generations.

Belief: **Nonprofit missions are best served by the nonprofit being financially sustainable.**
Chapter: Reframing Sustainability

Nonprofit organizations require financial resources to operate. Conventional thinking prioritizes the financial stability of a nonprofit over the achievement of the goals set forth in its mission. The assumption is that a mission cannot be realized without the long-term existence of the organization. This places the needs of the organization above those of the mission for which it was founded. As a result, most nonprofits are tasked with either building a large fundraising engine or developing a revenue model that mimics that of a for-profit company. While, at first blush, this may seem reasonable, in actuality it can restrict the creative exploration of other ways of sustainably accomplishing an organization's mission; focusing on financial needs may also delay deep engagement with that mission. What can get lost are some of the most effective ways of making change and completing the mission. In these cases, building a financial sustainability model is a distraction. In our case, a belief in focusing on finances above mission would place blinders on us, limiting our motivation to seek approaches that could support our goals to the benefit of many children.

Belief: **Failure marks a stopping point in the educational process.**
Chapter: Relearning Curiosity

This seems a ridiculous thing to say. We all have failed and have likely watched our children fail. A priority for ourselves and our children is that we learn from our failures and continue to move forward with resilience. Yet our educational systems are not structured with an orientation toward this kind of resilience. The typical school pattern is to instruct and then test; regardless of a student's success or failure, we move them on to new material. So, instruction continues regardless of whether learning is happening or mastery is achieved. An unspoken belief that many students internalize is that failure is the stopping point of learning. This is a case where a belief not only inhibits our goal of having children learn but it is also in direct conflict with another belief—that resilience is a quality to be cultivated.

Belief: **Educational opportunities are for those who meet the conditions of admission.**
Chapter: Relearning Curiosity

Admissions processes gate access to study at universities. Testing and admissions processes also often gate access to study in primary grades in low-income countries. There are a number of places where a low-cost private school is the alternative to a government school, and those private schools are often much more effective. Many governments do not have the ability to provide education for all, so they rely on a low-cost private school system to help. It is hard to argue that this belief does anything but limit the number of children you can reach. The whole point of an admissions process is to limit the number of students who have access to a particular educational system. While any given school may have its reasons for limiting the number of students who can attend, it is important that we don't build up a belief that applies to all educational opportunities. To do that would be in direct conflict with the UN's Sustainable Development Goal Number 4—to "ensure inclusive and equitable quality education and promote lifelong learning opportunities for all."

About the Author

With a background in science, technology, design, and entrepreneurship, Tinsley Galyean was the first to receive a PhD from the Interactive Cinema Group at the MIT Media Lab. He has developed interactive education projects with the Museum of Modern Art in New York; the Museum of Science in Boston; Liberty Science Center in Jersey City, New Jersey; the Georgia Aquarium in Atlanta; and Scitech in Perth, Australia. He has also developed media experiences for children through Disney and Warner Brothers and created an Emmy-nominated program for Discovery Kids. This work has led to numerous academic publications, patents, and the founding of four companies and two nonprofit organizations. As a board member and head of strategy, Tinsley had the privilege of helping to launch The Dalai Lama Center for Ethics and Transformative Values at MIT. While teaching at the MIT Media Lab, Tinsley cofounded Curious Learning—a global nonprofit using mobile technology to give everyone the opportunity to learn to read. He continues to serve as Curious Learning's CEO.

Tinsley travels extensively for work and pleasure, predominantly in and around low-income communities. When weather and work allow, you may find him sitting beside a lake in New Hampshire, working to not think about anything.

Index

www.ingramcontent.com/pod-product-compliance
Lightning Source LLC
Chambersburg PA
CBHW061315220326
41599CB00026B/4890